Deep
Point of View

A BUSY WRITER'S GUIDE

Marcy Kennedy

Tongue Untied Communications
ONTARIO, CANADA

Marcy Kennedy
marcykennedy@gmail.com
www.marcykennedy.com

Book Layout ©2013 BookDesignTemplates.com
Edited by Chris J. Saylor
Cover Design by Melinda VanLone

Point of View in Fiction/ Marcy Kennedy —1st ed.
ISBN 978-1-988069-04-3

Contents

iii

Why a Busy Writer's Guide?

A FEW YEARS AGO, I STARTED CREATING *Busy Writer's Guides* for a very simple reason—I wanted to give hope and practical help to writers who were struggling to reach their goals and dreams because of the demands life placed on them.

This became my passion because I know what it feels like to be overwhelmed by responsibilities that can't be ignored or delegated and to prioritize the needs of those I love over my own desires. I know what it feels like to make it through a day with no energy or creativity left to write.

And I knew I couldn't be the only one. The more writers I talked to, the more I found so many others who felt stretched too thin. They were trying to fit writing in around full-time jobs or around caring for children or aging parents or grandparents. They were battling physical and mental health problems. They had life commitments that were as important to them as writing.

They were people who wanted to achieve their dreams, but who didn't want to do it at the cost of their health, their relationships, or their moral compasses.

While I can't solve all the problems in the world, or in anyone's life, I wanted to help make writing a great book more achievable for those people—people like me.

And that's where the *Busy Writer's Guides* were born.

They're short, yet in-depth and practical. The intent is to give you the full coverage of a topic that you need to write well, but to do it in a way that still respects your time.

How does that work?

These guides leave out the filler and fancy prose padding meant to impress you. My goal isn't to make you think I'm fantastic. My goal is to help you become fantastic. I cut the fluff while keeping the substance so that you can have more time to write and more time to live your life.

Each book in the *Busy Writer's Guides* series gives you enough theory so that you can understand why things work and why they don't, but also enough examples to see how that theory looks in practice. Approaching it from two sides like this streamlines the learning process and speeds up your learning curve.

In addition, these guides provide tips and exercises to help you take what you've learned to the pages of your own story with an editor's-eye view. There's a leap we all need to make from intellectually understanding a topic to proficiently applying that topic to our work. The Take It to the Page sections give you a way to start, trying again to make this transition easier and quicker for you. If you're not ready to apply it to your work yet, you can skip these sections and come back to them later.

The final way that I try to respect your time is by separating some topics out into appendices. A lot of writing craft concepts overlap. I try my best to keep the material in the body of each of my books fresh. In other words, I minimize the content overlap between books as much as I can without sacrificing clarity. (In some cases, I still do have to re-explain elements or I wouldn't be doing justice to the concept at hand.)

When I think there are elements of other topics that aren't absolutely essential to understanding the current topic, but which would help you understand the topic of the current book better, I add them as appendices. That way, if you've read my other books and don't need a refresher, you can save time by skipping the appendices. If this is the first one of my books you've read, or if you want to refresh your memory on a topic, you can read the appendices.

And that's quite a long enough intro, I think. Time to get to the meat. If you want to find out more about me, you can visit my website at www.marcykennedy.com or check out the About the Author section at the end of this book.

CHAPTER ONE

Defining Deep POV

DEEP POV IS A SHORTENED WAY OF SAYING *deep penetration point of view*. It refers to the most intimate, closest writing style, where the reader experiences the story as if they were inside of the character—feeling what the character feels, experiencing what they experience, and hearing what they think—without any distance between them. It's emotionally intense and the author must stay completely invisible.

Deep POV was originally called close or intimate limited third-person point of view, and it first appeared and started gaining popularity between 1975 and 1995.

The reason for this steep rise in popularity is the connection deep POV creates between the reader and the viewpoint character. It makes the story interactive in a way that more distant approaches to point of view can't. It allows the reader to live vicariously through our viewpoint characters.

From a purely writing craft standpoint, when we master deep POV, we'll also have a stronger grasp on showing vs. telling and internal dialogue, and we'll be better able to avoid problems like backstory or info dump and point-of-view errors.

In this book, I'm going to help you understand deep POV better and learn how to apply it to your writing. To start, we need to look at how deep POV can improve our writing, come up with a working definition of what makes a passage deep POV, and dispel some of the biggest misconceptions about it.

HOW DEEP POV IMPROVES OUR WRITING

Since you picked up this book, you're probably already convinced about the value of deep POV. Just in case anyone ever challenges you, though, I want to give you a few of the many ways deep POV improves our writing.

Deep POV creates a stronger emotional connection.

The reader experiences the story from the inside out because they're inside the character. A shallower POV creates an experience from the outside in—we're looking at the character externally. The difference is like that between feeling your own emotions and watching someone else's.

Deep POV eliminates unintentional telling.

Show, don't tell is one of those foundational writing guidelines that show up in every "best writing tips" list. Properly executing that advice becomes more challenging, but if you master deep POV, you'll also improve your grasp of showing. This doesn't mean you'll never tell. It means you'll better understand when to show and when to tell, and you won't accidentally default to telling.

Deep POV feels tighter and quicker in pace even though it often uses more words.

Tight writing is less about the number of words used and more about making every word count. Deep POV cuts out a lot of the filler words and emotionally empty words and replaces them with strong words that hold the reader's interest. When they're interested, the book feels faster-paced.

Deep POV helps the reader forget that they're reading.

Emotional depth, connection to the viewpoint character, smooth writing, and a fast pace all combine to form a reading experience that blocks out the world around us. We no longer consciously see the words on the page and instead vicariously live the story.

Now that we know a few of the reasons and can better explain our choice should we be asked, it's time to define deep POV.

WHAT DEFINES A DEEP POV PASSAGE?

It's almost impossible to hit a target if we don't know what we're aiming for. We might accidentally get lucky, but that's no way to write a book. Writing a book takes too much time to depend on hoping for lucky accidents.

Because of that, we need a practical definition of what sets deep POV apart from other writing styles. Once we know what type of writing qualifies as deep POV, we can work on developing it in our writing.

Deep POV is defined by the following aspects:

1. Limited knowledge
2. Inside-out perspective
3. Interior life
4. Interpretations

5. Immediacy

I'll give you a quick overview of these elements now, and then we'll spend the rest of the book exploring them.

Limited Knowledge

While we're writing in deep POV, we're constrained. Before that terminology turns you away from this technique, consider this—we're constrained in the same way that we're constrained by our body in life. It binds us to one physical place at a time. We experience life through the medium of our body—our eyes, our ears, our nose, our mouths, our skin, our minds.

When we're writing in deep POV, we'll be sharing what a single character knows and experiences at a single point in time. That does limit what we can show and when we can show it, but our stories become richer for it.

Inside-Out Perspective

Limited knowledge alone doesn't fully create deep POV. Shallower points of view can share that quality. It's one part of the whole. Along with limited knowledge, we also need to shift the perspective of the story so that we share it from the inside out.

As readers, we're not simply experiencing the story along with the viewpoint character. We *become* the viewpoint character. We climb inside their mind and body.

From the writing side, this is a fundamental shift. When we share the story from the inside out, rather than from the outside in, what we share and the language we use to share it will change. Filtering and distancing words will have no place. We'll have to consider the "eye" of the narrative. From the outside in, we might write *a frown crossed her face.* But from the inside out, we'd say *she frowned.*

The first sees our viewpoint character from the outside. The second acts from inside her.

Interior Life

In the same way that limited knowledge alone wasn't enough, neither is switching the perspective to come from the inside. We could share the story from the inside out and still not capture deep POV if we leave out the interior life. The interior life includes motivations, internal dialogue (character thoughts), and visceral, instinctive bodily reactions.

Interpretations

Another way of phrasing this would be judgments, but I didn't want to use that terminology because it's too easily confused with being judgmental. We don't need to create judgmental characters to write in deep POV. We do need the entire story to be an interpretation of events rather than an unbiased report of them.

Interpretation means that the story is reported through our viewpoint character's rose-colored glasses or violet-colored glasses or gray-colored glasses. They have opinions on what they experience. Everything on the page comes through them and is phrased the way they'd phrase it and shown based on what they notice and how they think about it. Everything.

Immediacy

Immediacy means that we're experiencing the story in "real time." When we're reading, the events play out in front of us as if we were watching them at the same time as they're happing.

This isn't a matter of tense. This feeling can be created in a story written in past tense just as well as it can in a story written in present tense. Word choice, showing rather than telling, and carefully managing cause and effect create immediacy in our writing.

Combined with an inside-out perspective, immediacy helps create the feeling that there's no distance between the viewpoint character and the reader.

MISCONCEPTIONS ABOUT DEEP POV

Myths and misunderstandings abound no matter what skill we're trying to learn. An important part of learning is sorting out the misinformation surrounding a topic. So before I start explaining how to develop deep POV in our writing, I want to talk about what it *isn't*.

Misconception #1 – You need to write in first person to write deep POV.

Deep POV isn't about pronouns. We can write deep POV from a third-person point of view. And we haven't necessarily created a more intimate story by writing in first person rather than third person.

Misconception #2 – You create deep POV by spending a lot of time on internal dialogue.

This is possibly one of the most dangerous misconceptions about writing in deep POV because it can lead us to include too much internal dialogue (character thoughts) within our stories. Books written in deep POV usually will include more internal dialogue than a book written in a more distant POV, but that internal dialogue still needs to be seamlessly woven in with action, description, and dialogue. We shouldn't allow our stories to stall out by dropping in giant chunks of internal dialogue.

This isn't the only issue with this misconception, though. As I've already pointed out, deep POV is about more than simply internal dialogue. It's also about internal, visceral reactions to what our viewpoint character experiences. It's about creating a feeling of immediacy, as if we're watching the story play out in front of us as it happens (regardless of the tense used). We'll look at this more later.

Misconception #3 – Deep POV requires us to put our internal dialogue in italics.

Point of view can be a confusing topic for writers because of how closely it ties to showing vs. telling and internal dialogue. Whether or not to italicize internal dialogue is a question of formatting and not one of whether you're writing in a deep or shallow point of view.

The guidelines for italicizing our internal dialogue are outside the scope of this book, but generally speaking, we'll have less italicized internal dialogue in a book written in deep POV than we will in a book written in a shallower POV.

This is because we only italicize internal dialogue when it's what's called direct internal dialogue. Direct internal dialogue is written in first-person present tense regardless of the tense and person of the rest of the story. Because they're italicized, they draw attention to themselves.

In deep POV, we're so close inside the character that the character's thoughts tend to flow and interweave with the rest of the writing and are best written in the same person and tense as the story itself. To explain this another way, the less the internal dialogue draws attention to itself, the more immersed the reader feels in the character. The less attention the internal dialogue draws to itself, the closer the reader feels.

(If you want to learn more about direct vs. indirect internal dialogue, read Appendix A.)

Misconception #4 – Deep POV means we have to show everything that happens.

One argument I've heard against deep POV is that it will make your story too long and feel too slow because you need to show everything that happens and you can't summarize.

Let me give you an example. You might write something like this...

> They gathered up their belongings.

Or something like...

> They ran two red lights on the drive to Brenda's house.

According to this misconception of deep POV, you wouldn't be able to write either of those sentences in a deep POV book. You'd need to show them collecting every single item or you'd have to show the entire drive.

Deep POV doesn't mean you show everything that happens in a stream of consciousness-style narrative. Deep POV is an overarching technique we can use in our writing, but we can still pull back and use moments of narrative summary to skim unimportant information when necessary. We can also cut any internal dialogue that would bore the reader. Deep POV is a tool, not a straightjacket.

Now that we have a clearer understanding of what deep POV can do for our story, and what doesn't make a passage deep POV, I'm going to explain the point-of-view options we have as writers. If we want to write in deep POV, that choice eliminates some point-of-view options and helps us focus.

CHAPTER TWO

Understanding Our Point-of-View Options

I N ORDER TO FULLY UNDERSTAND DEEP POV, we first need to understand point of view in general. So before we move into the practical techniques for creating deep POV, I'm going to give you a point-of-view refresher. I recommend that you read this chapter even if you're familiar with point of view already because I'm going to be discussing the topic as it relates to deep POV. In other words, I'm going to be using the other point-of-view options to also give you a better understanding of deep POV.

(If you're newer to writing and you don't already have a foundational understanding of point of view, then I strongly recommend that you grab a copy of my book *Point of View in Fiction* and read that first. It'll make understanding and executing deep POV much easier in the end.)

DEFINING POINT OF VIEW

Point of view is all about perspective. It's the voice telling the story. It's the eyes and mind we're experiencing the story through. It's the opinion that's coloring every element included within the story.

Definition: _Point of view is a position or perspective from which something is considered or evaluated; a standpoint (Merriam-Webster Dictionary)._

THE FOUR TYPES OF POINT OF VIEW

Point of view (POV) comes in four basic types: first person, second person, third person, and omniscient.

Omniscient Point of View

In omniscient POV, an all-knowing narrator tells the story. This narrator isn't a character in the story. Usually the narrator is the author, but the narrator can, more rarely, also be a created character like Death in *The Book Thief.*

Deep POV is impossible in an omniscient book. They're on opposite ends of the narrative spectrum when defining how close the reader is to the characters. In omniscient POV, the voice we hear is that of the omniscient narrator. It's their perspective we receive on events. The opinions and judgments about the situation in the story belong to the omniscient narrator.

The omniscient narrator is the only viewpoint in the story. Even though they can tell us what a character is thinking or feeling, we're receiving those thoughts and feelings second-hand, filtered through the omniscient narrator. We don't experience them alongside the character. We don't hear the character's voice, unless we're writing dialogue or an isolated line of direct internal dialogue. We're distant from the characters because we're functionally standing next to the omniscient narrator, listening to them tell us a story.

(For an explanation of the difference between direct and indirect internal dialogue, please read Appendix A.)

Definition: *Omniscience is having infinite awareness, understanding, and insight; being possessed of universal or complete knowledge (Merriam-Webster Dictionary).*

Second-Person Point of View

In second-person POV, the narrator is a *you*. Second-person POV can be written in deep POV, but it's an unpopular point of view. Generally, only choose-your-own-adventure-style stories use second-person POV. I won't be discussing it further in this book. If you want a slightly longer discussion of second-person POV, I recommend you read *Point of View in Fiction: A Busy Writer's Guide.*

Third-Person Point of View

Third-person POV uses the pronouns *he* and *she*. The narrator is a character (or characters) within the story, and as the reader, we generally hear the story told in their voices, not in the author's voice. Within a scene or chapter, we should be inside a single character. If we switch viewpoint characters without a proper transition, it's called head-hopping, a major POV error. Chapter breaks and scene breaks are the most commonly accepted proper transitions.

Narrative distance, though, is a continuum. On one end of that continuum lies deep POV. Third person allows you to slide along that continuum depending on what genre you're writing in, your personal style, and the needs of your story. Writing in a more distant third person doesn't give us permission to head-hop or insert information that our viewpoint character couldn't have known. What distance does is change the feel of our writing and, to some extent, the voice we hear. A farther narrative distance creates a cooler tone, while a closer narrative distance gives our writing a more intense, intimate feel. A farther narrative distance allows the reader to hear the author more, while a closer narrator distance sticks tightly to the viewpoint character's voice.

First-Person Point of View

In first-person POV, the narrator is a character within the story as well. They use pronouns like *I, me, we, us, mine,* and *ours.* Just like it sounds, in first person, the character is telling us the story directly.

First-person POV comes with a tricky element to it. It can be written in present tense, in past tense as a retrospective narrator, or in past tense that's treated as functionally identical to a third-person past tense story. The choice we make here determines how we can use deep POV in our writing.

When writing in present tense or when writing in past tense that's treated functionally identical to a third-person past tense story (in that the viewpoint character/narrator has no knowledge of how the story will turn out), the only difference between a story written in third person with deep POV and a story written in an intimate first-person POV is the pronouns.

A common misconception I mentioned earlier is that, if you write in first-person POV, you're automatically writing in deep POV. First-person POV tends to have less wiggle room on the narrative distance spectrum than third-person POV. However, it can also be stripped of the immediacy, internal reactions, and interpretations that define deep POV. To put this another way, if you're writing in first-person POV, you need to understand and apply deep POV techniques, too. Don't assume that your first-person POV is working the way you want it to simply because the pronoun you're using is *I* rather than *he* or *she*.

A retrospective first-person narrator is different. They tell the story from some point in the future. They already know how the story turns out, and so the story they're giving to the reader isn't just the events as they experienced them. It's also their interpretation of those events and of their younger selves from a different perspective created by time. They're both in the story as the viewpoint character and outside of the story as the narrator.

This makes a retrospective first-person narrator the most difficult to handle when it comes to deep POV. They're actually a hybrid. Some elements of deep POV will be there (specifically the interior life and interpretations), but other elements (like the limited knowledge) will be missing. The inside-out perspective and the immediacy will come and go based on the needs of the story and the preference of the author.

If you're new to deep POV or new to writing in first person, I recommend staying away from a retrospective first-person narrator. Once you've mastered both, you'll be better able to handle the unique challenges presented by writing a first-person retrospective story in deep POV.

GUIDES VS. FILTERS

In an article she wrote for *The Internet Review of Science Fiction*, Juliette Wade described the difference in narrators as guides vs. filters. I felt that was such a wonderful way of explaining it that I wanted to share it with you, but all credit for the terms as categories is due to Juliette. (Her article is called "Point of View: Reading Beyond the I's." It's based on linguistics and pragmatics, and it's very interesting, but if grammar makes you cringe, you'll probably want to avoid it.)

A guide narrator is someone who is external to the story in some way. Omniscient narrators and first-person retrospective narrators fall into this category. They're aware that the reader exists and that they're telling that reader a story. This means that they're guiding us through that story, showing us what they want us to see and explaining things in a way that fits their agenda.

A filter narrator, on the other hand, is not external to the story. Close third-person narrators and other first-person narrators are filter narrators. They don't know the reader exists. They're not telling a story. They're living their life, and everything the reader receives flows through them and is influenced by them in a non-self-conscious way. They might lie to themselves and lie to other characters in the story, but they can't lie to the reader.

A true deep POV narrative can only happen when the narrator is a filter.

In the remainder of this book, we're going to learn how to write a non-retrospective first-person story or third-person story in deep POV.

CHAPTER THREE

Big-Picture Guidelines

A S WE START ON OUR JOURNEY INTO DEEP POV, we need to deal with the big picture guidelines first. These are either items that are generally good advice for fiction writing but are essential when it comes to deep POV, or they're ways that writing in deep POV differs slightly from conventional writing wisdom.

LIMIT THE NUMBER OF VIEWPOINT CHARACTERS

Keeping your viewpoint characters to a minimum is good advice overall, but it becomes especially important when you're writing in deep POV.

Deep POV means your voice is functionally invisible. The viewpoint character's voice replaces it. So for every viewpoint character you introduce, you need to create a distinct voice and view of the world to go along with it. The more viewpoint characters you have, the more difficult it becomes to differentiate sufficiently between them.

By making a character a viewpoint character, we're also asking the reader to invest emotionally in them. We're asking them to care at a higher level than for a non-viewpoint character. The more characters we present for them to care about this deeply, the harder it becomes for them to do so because they spend less time in each character's viewpoint. Think about this in terms of relationships in our lives. The more time we invest in a relationship, the stronger and closer that relationship is likely to become. We'll know that person better the more time we spend with them.

I'm not saying you can't use a large number of viewpoint characters when writing in deep POV, but you need to understand the consequences of trying it. The more viewpoint characters we have, the more confusing our book can become, the more difficult it becomes to write well, and the less attached the reader will be to any single character.

I talk in depth in *Point of View in Fiction* on how to decide on the number of viewpoint characters we include in our stories, but when it comes to deep POV stories, my general recommendation is three or fewer. If we include three, the normal choices will be our protagonist, our antagonist, and our most important secondary character (often the love interest).

NO BATON PASSES

A baton pass is a type of transition where we move the viewpoint from one character to another using an object to signal the shift.

I'll give you an example so you can see it in practice. The baton pass is bolded.

Allison loaded the pistol and flicked off the safety. This might be the stupidest mistake of her life—the man injured himself trying to open a can of tomato sauce—but she needed someone to cover her. "Use both hands when you shoot. This isn't TV."

She passed him the gun.

Mark wrapped his hands around the grip, still warm from Allison's palms. The coil of tension in his stomach melted away like it was sugar in the rain. All those lunch hours he'd spent at the shooting range with the idea of surprising her on her birthday now seemed prophetic. He could handle this. For once, he could protect her instead of the other way around.

Occasionally, you'll see big-name authors or authors writing in a far narrative distance use a baton pass. Just because they sometimes get away with it doesn't mean we should try. It doesn't even mean they should.

Many people, myself included, consider a baton pass to be an improper point-of-view transition. It causes the reader to hesitate and can confuse them. In other words, it breaks the fictional dream and shoves them out of the story.

If you're writing in deep POV, using a baton pass is an exceptionally unwise decision for those reasons. You violate deep POV and your reader will feel disoriented and whiplashed, especially if they miss the baton pass cue (a common occurrence).

When we need to change viewpoint characters, we need to do it using a proper break—a chapter break, a scene break, or a mid-scene shift using a blank line or symbolic divider.

WE CAN'T HIDE INFORMATION FROM THE READER IF OUR VIEWPOINT CHARACTER KNOWS IT

We shouldn't normally hide known information anyway because it can lead to readers feeling tricked, and a reader who feels manipulated is often a disgruntled reader. In deep POV, however, this becomes a central tenant. If our viewpoint character knows about something and would naturally think about that thing, we can't withhold that information from the reader.

We're now into tricky territory where writers can easily become confused. Two types of withholding happen in a story—one good and one bad.

The good type of information to hide or withhold is backstory. Even though our viewpoint character knows their own past, those events stay in their subconscious unless something external in the present day triggers them. This is true to real life and, therefore, true to writing in deep POV. Most of us don't sit around thinking, in detail, about something that happened to us five years ago. We also don't tend to openly share our history with someone we've just met.

When we have our characters share their backstory too early or without the proper provocation, we've shared when we should have withheld. When it comes to sharing this type of information, remember these three guidelines—we need an external cause before we share the backstory (through dialogue or internal dialogue), we should share it in small bits, and we should only share it when it becomes important to the present-day story.

The bad type of information to withhold is facts known by our viewpoint character, realizations our viewpoint character comes to, or other pieces of vital information held back for the sole purpose of creating suspense in the reader. If our viewpoint character would think about something significant to the story, we need to share it. (Knowing this information and wondering what will happen next actually creates more and better tension in the reader than leaving them in the dark.)

When they figure out the identity of the murderer, for example, you can't tell the reader they figured it out but continue to hide the murderer's identity. Doing so violates deep POV. If your viewpoint character knows they themselves are the murderer, you can't withhold that from the reader. If your character is delusional and has had a break with reality because he can't face what he's done, then you could hide the truth, *but only because the character himself is no longer aware of the truth.* In that case, you'd lay out hints for the reader so that they won't feel wrongly deceived when the truth comes out.

If you're writing in a more distant POV, you have more freedom in what you share and what you withhold.

AVOID DIRECT INTERNAL DIALOGUE

I mentioned this briefly when I talked about the common misconceptions surrounding deep POV. It's important enough for me to cover it in full. (I'll be talking about direct and indirect internal dialogue a bit here, but for more in-depth coverage, take a look at Appendix A.)

In most fiction, we can (and often should) use both direct and indirect internal dialogue. In deep POV, the less direct internal dialogue we use, the better.

I'll explain.

Direct internal dialogue is in present tense, is in first person, and is normally italicized.

Angela dove behind the nearest tree. *Crap. He saw me. I'm sure he saw me.*

By its very nature, direct internal dialogue calls attention to it-self. It's set apart from the rest of the writing. It's different. When we use direct internal dialogue, we're saying that this particular line or lines is more in the character's voice than the rest of the story.

But when we're writing in deep POV, it's all supposed to be in the viewpoint character's voice. The reader is already hearing things phrased the way they would phrase them. So there's no need to set their thoughts apart from everything else.

Think about this in terms of how you go about your day. There's no clear distinction between *I'm thinking now* and *Now I'm not think-ing*. We're almost always thinking, and our thoughts weave throughout our day and our actions.

It's the same for fiction written in deep POV. Anything that isn't a description (of action, visceral reactions, setting, etc.) or dialogue is technically internal dialogue—our character thinking to themselves and mentally interacting with the world. It will feel deeper and more natural if we don't set portions of their thoughts apart as something special.

ANCHOR THE VIEWPOINT CHARACTER IMMEDIATELY

Like many of the points above, this advice is sound even if you're not writing in deep POV. In deep POV, however, it's a necessity. We need to ground the reader within the viewpoint character as soon as possible.

Ideally, we want to do this within the first sentence of every sce-ne if our book has more than one viewpoint character. Remember, in deep POV, the reader experiences the whole story from inside of a character. This means they need to know who they're inside of right away or they'll feel lost, confused, and/or disconnected from the story.

The easiest way to anchor the reader within the viewpoint character is to share a physical sensation. For example...

Scott's stomach knotted, and he lunged for the door.

In this example, the viewpoint character must be Scott. No one else can be aware of what he's feeling inside. Any time we share something that only one character could be aware of, it acts as a cue to the reader that this is the person whose body we'll be sharing.

We could also use an action coupled with thoughts to cue the reader.

Scott pounded on the door. They couldn't hold him here against his will. He had rights.

This works the same way as an internal sensation. No one knows what Scott is thinking except Scott; therefore, Scott must be the viewpoint character.

In books with two viewpoint characters where we regularly switch back and forth between them, we earn more flexibility the further we go into the book. Once the reader knows that there are only two viewpoints, they'll expect one of those two to always be the viewpoint character. They'll attach to the first one we mention in each new scene, whether or not we share anything internal from that character. This helps us, but also means we have to be extra vigilant about unintentional ambiguity.

If our book has only one viewpoint character, then anchoring the reader immediately isn't really a concern. What we need to remember in this case is to alternate between internals and externals in order to keep the reader connected with both our character and the world around them.

CHAPTER FOUR

Limited Knowledge

I N CHAPTER ONE, I SAID THAT LIMITED knowledge means we'll be sharing what a single character knows and experiences at a single point in time.

How do we achieve this? **We become the viewpoint character.**

That might sounds strange at first. What I mean by that is we need to think about our viewpoint character and what they know and experience in terms of what we can know and experience.

As I take you through the ways to create limited knowledge, we're also going to look at how this mirrors the way we live our lives. At the end of the chapter, I'll share how looking at it from this perspective also helps us when we're not sure if we've broken deep POV.

DON'T SHARE THOUGHTS, FEELINGS, OR MOTIVATIONS THAT BELONG TO NON-VIEWPOINT CHARACTERS

We know our own thoughts, feelings, and motivations. We don't know anyone else's. Understanding that our viewpoint character is just like us in that their perception is limited to their own thoughts, feelings, and motivations is foundational to avoiding point-of-view errors and to staying in deep POV.

Time for a closer look and some examples of how we can make mistakes in this area, and then I'll show you how to work around it.

We can't know how someone else is feeling.

They might be smiling on the outside and in agony on the inside. Or the scowl I interpret as anger toward me might simply be gas pains. So when we write something like the following example, we're violating deep POV. (In this example, Dan is **not** our viewpoint character.)

> Dan kept his attention on the bomb, unfazed by the ticking clock.

Our viewpoint character can't know whether Dan is fazed or unfazed. Dan might seem unfazed on the outside, but inside he might be struggling not to throw up or pass out.

Some writers might argue "but that's my viewpoint character's opinion, so I'm not violating deep POV." Keep in mind—we aren't there to explain this to the reader or to defend anything. All they know is whether something feels right or not. And the example above feels distant and like telling. We'll look at this more when I give you some solutions later on.

We can't know what anyone else is thinking, or even if they're thinking about anything at all.

We'll start with an obvious example. This one would fall into the category of head-hopping (the cardinal point-of-view sin). For this example, we'll introduce a character named Ellie to join Dan.

Ellie paced the floor behind Dan, trying to keep out of his way yet unable to hold still. Dan didn't look up, but he wished she'd freeze for just one minute so he could think.

In the first sentence, we're inside Ellie, and then we switch to hearing what Dan's thinking in the second sentence. This would violate deep POV no matter which of the two was supposed to be our viewpoint character.

I want to share one more for this section because it's one I see frequently in my editing work. This one is sneakier. Ellie's our viewpoint character this time.

Ellie grabbed his arm. "If I spot the bomb first, I won't know how to defuse it. We'll lose time trying to find each other again."
Dan thought about that for a minute. "Alright. We'll stick together."

We've violated deep POV when we say "Dan thought about that." Ellie doesn't know that Dan is thinking about what she said.

In addition, not only is this a violation of deep POV, but it's telling rather than showing, and they're empty words in that they don't add anything to our understanding of the character or the situation. They don't add anything to the reader's experience.

The solution is to show the reader evidence that Dan might be thinking.

For example...

Dan rubbed his temples. "Alright. We'll stick together."

The reader can fill in the blanks (they're smart that way) and guess that Dan was thinking while rubbing his temples. This also shows them something about Dan. The man who rubs his temples before agreeing is a different man from the one who scowls at her before agreeing. Within the subtext, the former feels worried about the situation and the time ticking away, while the latter seems annoyed at Ellie and her perceived neediness.

We can't know why someone acts in a certain way.

For example, say you turned toward me. I can't know if you turned toward me because you heard me enter the room, because you caught a glimpse of me from the corner of your eye, or because you were going to turn that direction anyway.

Likewise, in our books, our viewpoint character can guess at another character's motivation, but they can't know it. If they're guessing, then it should be clear from the way we write it that this is a guess or assumption. If we state it as a fact, we've violated deep POV.

So, if we're still in Ellie's viewpoint, and we write something like the sentence that follows, we're committing an error.

Dan grabbed the signed baseball to keep it away from her.

(I'll leave deciding why Dan is playing with a signed baseball when he should be hunting a bomb up to your imagination.)

By sharing his motivation for grabbing the baseball, we've created a POV error and violated deep POV. Ellie can't know why Dan grabbed the baseball. Maybe he wanted a closer look at it to see if the signature was smudged. Maybe holding it makes him feel more confident. Maybe he's going to throw the baseball at her because she lost his bomb-defusing tools. And, yes, maybe he grabbed it to keep it away from her. The point is, she can't know Dan's motivation because her knowledge is limited.

So how do we fix situations like these so we don't violate deep POV?

We have three main options for dealing with spots where we've accidentally turned our viewpoint character into a telepath or an empath.

Allow the reader to fill in the blanks using the context.

In other words, take out the problematic phrase and leave only the objective description of the event.

Whenever possible, this is the best option for resolving all point-of-view errors, not just errors in deep POV. In my book *Showing and Telling in Fiction*, I explained that the difference between showing and telling is that showing gives the evidence and telling dictates a conclusion. (See Appendix B for a longer explanation of the two.) We can apply the same principle here. Show the reader the evidence and allow them to draw a conclusion from it rather than dictating a conclusion for them.

Let's take a quick look at how this plays out in an example. We'll stick with Dan and Ellie. Ellie is still our viewpoint character.

> "I think..." Ellie rubbed her hands up and down her jeans. She'd always imagined that, if Ben came after her, it'd be with a car bomb. She'd never dreamed he might take out a whole building of people to punish her. "This might be my fault. I might be the target."
>
> Dan's eyes narrowed with suspicion. "What do you mean?"

With suspicion is an error. And we don't even need it. Watch.

"I think..." Ellie rubbed her hands up and down her jeans. She'd always imagined that, if Ben came after her, it'd be with a car bomb. She'd never dreamed he might take out a whole building of people to punish her. "This might be my fault. I might be the target."

Dan's eyes narrowed. "What do you mean?"

Sometimes, correcting the error will require us to add or change a little more in the way of context to make sure the emotion or motivation is clear. The most common additions or changes will involve body language and dialogue.

Make it clear the viewpoint character is interpreting.

Our viewpoint character can (and will) often make a guess or interpret based on the evidence they see. What makes the difference between violating deep POV and staying soundly within it is how we handle this information.

Let's go back to one of our original examples.

Dan kept his attention on the bomb, unfazed by the ticking clock.

If we meant for this to be our viewpoint character's opinion, then we need to make that clear.

Ellie's mouth dried out and no amount of swallowing eased the tight feeling in her throat. She paced back and forth. Every time she tried to stop, shaking threatened to collapse her knees.

Dan pulled delicate tools she couldn't hope to name from his belt and removed the bomb's casing. His hands didn't even tremble.

She wiped her sweating palms on her jeans. It was like watching the doctors on *Grey's Anatomy* debate their love lives and banter while slicing into the most fragile parts of the human body. How could anyone stay so calm when lives depended on each cut they made?

After this fleshed-out example, we still know that Dan seemed unfazed. We also know that this is Ellie's opinion on his reaction compared to hers. She might be right. Defusing bombs could come as easily to him as driving a car. She might be wrong. Part of the fun of deep POV is that our viewpoint characters might be mistaken in their interpretation. (That's not quite as fun when it happens to us in real life.)

Show how the viewpoint character knows something that would otherwise be considered an error.

This is an extension of the last solution. In this solution, the viewpoint character is still going to be interpreting, but it's more like an educated guess, so they're also going to share why they've come to this conclusion.

In this example, Ellie is going to state that Dan is lying to her. What makes it work is that she also shows the evidence of how she draws that conclusion.

> Dan's hands hovered over the wires, but he didn't make a cut.
> Ellie inched closer. "What's wrong?"
> "Nothing. Just measuring twice."
> He shot her that cocky grin of his, but his gaze twitched away from her—so quick it almost wasn't there. She'd seen that same tell a thousand times when a story source fudged the truth. He was lying to her. Something was very, very wrong.

We need to be careful with this because we're doubling up on showing and telling. Technically, showing and telling the same thing is repetitious, but when it's used strategically, in moments when we want to emphasize an important element, it can work well.

I know that was a long first point for how our viewpoint character's knowledge is limited, but it was an important one. The rest are shorter.

DON'T SHARE THINGS OUTSIDE OF THE VIEWPOINT CHARACTER'S SIGHT, EARSHOT, OR SMELL RANGE

Sounds obvious, right? But sometimes we forget to think about how we perceive the world around us. In the examples below, our viewpoint character is a woman named Janice.

We can't see something that's happening behind us or that's happening when our eyes are closed. Yet sometimes in our fiction we'll write something like this.

> Janice turned her back to him. He stuck out his tongue and stomped off.

Unless Janice can see through the back of her skull, she can't see him stick out his tongue at her.

If we don't notice something happening, we can't comment on it or tell someone else about it. We're completely unaware of it.

When we're writing, we sometimes accidentally show the reader an action another character did that our viewpoint character didn't notice, or we'll share something our viewpoint character themselves is doing that they aren't aware of at the time. Both are wrong when we're writing in deep POV.

> Janice didn't realize she was tearing the tissue into thin strips.

Because she didn't realize it, we can't write it down. She's our eyes in the world.

But...but...but what if that unconscious action is essential? That's fine. Include it when the viewpoint character does become aware of it.

> Janice reached for her tissue, but a pile of shredded pieces met her fingers. When had she done that?

We can't normally see our own face or anything on our back half either.

This is an easy element to confuse. We know when our face moves (that's an action), but we can't see, for example, if our eyes are sparkling. (And that's only one reason we should never write about sparkly eyes—don't get me started on the others.)

We don't know if the shade of blue in our eyes darkens. We can't know if we have five red lash marks down our back. (If you've ever had an injury where there are multiple wounds in an area, you'll know that you can't distinguish the wounds enough to count them.)

We also don't know what's happening across town, across the world, or even in another room in our house.

So if our viewpoint character can't see it, hear it, touch it, taste it, or smell it *at that moment*, we can't include it. If we do, it's a point-of-view error and we've left deep POV.

DON'T SHARE EVENTS BEFORE THEY HAPPEN

We don't know what our future holds, and we can't experience something before it actually happens. Yet on the page we easily slip into showing the future before it takes place.

Writers violate deep POV in this way for a couple of reasons. The first is we might be trying to increase suspense, but having a "little did she know" moment is a cheap and lazy way to build suspense. If the suspense isn't there naturally, then we have a bigger structural problem that we need to fix. Telling the reader that something important is coming doesn't make up for the lack of organic suspense in our plot. The solution is to go back to see how we can hint at it in a way that feels natural to the story world.

And that leads in to the second way that writers might accidentally fall into breaking deep POV by sharing things before they happen. We might be confused about the difference between foreshadowing and forecasting (also called foretelling).

Foreshadowing is a good thing. In foreshadowing, you drop subtle hints for the reader of what might be coming in the future. For example, maybe the climax of our story hinges on our protagonist's skills with a knife. Earlier in the story, we'd lay the groundwork for this by showing them sharpening their knife collection, whittling a toy for the neighbor's child, and tossing their knife into the air, catching it by the handle every time. Our main character could also notice something just in passing that becomes important later in the story. Foreshadowing makes our story feel richer and better developed.

In forecasting, you tell the reader what's coming or you tell them that something important is coming even if you don't tell them what it is. I call this little-did-she-know syndrome, but we don't actually have to use the words "little did she/he know" for it to be forecasting. Forecasting is a bad thing.

I'll give you a few examples of possible ways a writer might forecast. These are by no means exhaustive, since forecasting can take many forms, but I wanted to give you an idea of the feel and flavor they have.

Imagine these as the last line of a chapter or a scene.

She never saw her again.

That was the last good day they'd have for a long time.

If she'd known then the changes that small act would bring, she never would have gotten out of bed that morning.

All of those sentences come from outside the character and are things the viewpoint character couldn't have known. They don't belong in deep POV.

The third reason we accidentally share things before they happen is we simply didn't think about the fact that things "happen" in the order that we place them on the page.

So when we describe how someone speaks before our viewpoint character hears them speak, we've violated deep POV. For example...

His voice turned hard. "How did you know that?"

Whenever we're confused about this element of deep POV, we can ask ourselves *when would I have experienced this if I were a character in the story?*

That's the moment when it should appear on the page.

AVOID HAVING YOUR VIEWPOINT CHARACTER THINK ABOUT THINGS THEY'RE FAMILIAR WITH

There are parts of my life that I never think about, and I'd bet there are parts of your life that you don't think about, either. Yet sometimes all those elements sneak into our writing, creating POV errors and taking us out of deep POV.

You probably don't think about your eye color, or the way your living room looks (unless you come home to find that someone robbed you or your dog ate the couch cushions), or about the clothes your boss normally wears.

You don't think about how to drive your car or work your cell phone.

In our story, say we have a scientist who knows all about how her complicated piece of equipment runs, why they use it for this particular test, and so on. If we have her thinking about and "explaining" to herself elements that she takes for granted, we've violated deep POV.

We don't think about the setup of our society, either—we take that for granted.

Let's say a man with green skin who is riding a bicycle nearly runs into our viewpoint character. Whether our viewpoint character reacts to the fact that the man has green skin or the fact that they were nearly bicycle roadkill tells us a lot about the story world.

If our viewpoint character reacts to the green skin, then the reader will know that's weird in this world. If our viewpoint character doesn't react to the green skin, then the reader knows green-skinned people are common in this society.

Where we can sometimes make a mistake is if we have our character react to the green skin even if it's common. Unfortunately, we don't pay special attention to things we experience all the time.

We also don't think about how we're related to people. Have you ever written something like this?

Her best friend, Meighan, waved from across the street.

Jimmy, her little brother, grabbed the letter from her hand.

Our viewpoint character already knows how they're related to the other character. They have no reason to think about it, which means that including it violates deep POV.

And yes, some of these elements might be essential for the reader to understand. We'll need to find a way to work them in without violating deep POV. If we want to mention an element of society, for example, we could break that element, so that something the character normally takes for granted isn't working. Or we could have them be angry with the way their society is and therefore think about how they want to change it. To return to our biker example, perhaps our viewpoint character feels the green-skinned "race" is entitled and that the biker who nearly ran our character down is evidence of that.

However, most of the time, those elements we want to include aren't actually essential, and deep POV forces us to consider what's truly important to our story and what isn't. The story will be stronger for it.

(If you want to learn more about this topic, check out Appendix C.)

DON'T MAGICALLY FILL GAPS IN YOUR CHARACTER'S KNOWLEDGE

As you might have noticed, most of these points are easy for us to get wrong as writers if we're not paying attention to them. Yet, when we keep *you are the viewpoint character* in mind, it enhances our writing in vast ways by making the world feel more real and the viewpoint character feel more like the one through whom we're experiencing the story. This is equally true for knowledge gaps.

How about an example for this point? If I lifted the hood of my car, I could *probably* tell you which piece of metal was the engine. After that, I couldn't name anything. If we have a character like me, and she pops the hood of her car, all she'll see is tubes and pieces of metal. She won't be able to name the piece that's smoking or rattling.

If our character doesn't know the name of the parts of a saddle, what to call pieces of scientific equipment, or even a person's name, we can't give the proper name for those items or people. Until they learn what to call it, they'll come up with some designation of their own.

You've probably experienced this yourself in a situation as simple as a buffet where you ask a server something like "What's that green thing there?" We all have gaps in our knowledge. So will our characters. Leave the gaps until such a time as they're naturally filled.

USE THE CORRECT ARTICLE DEPENDING ON WHETHER SOMETHING IS KNOWN OR UNKNOWN

Articles are an easy part of the English language to underestimate, but they're an important element for showing what our character knows and avoiding accidentally describing the situation based on our knowledge as the author.

The indicates something known—a person, an object, or information that we're already familiar with.

A or *an* indicates new information, something we're just noticing or discovering for the first time.

I'll give you an example so you can see how this can cause problems in deep POV. I'll put the important article in bold and italics.

> Alexis crept down the darkened hallway. She wiggled the knob on the first door on her left, and the door swung open. She ducked into the room, flicked on her flashlight, and swept the room with the beam. The light glinted off the metal front of ***the*** safe.

Sounds fine, right? It might be, but it might not be.

Was Alexis looking for this specific safe? If she was, no problem. She knew a safe was in the building, she went hunting for it, and she was lucky enough to find it.

But if Alexis didn't know the safe was there, we have a problem. Say, for example, that she was looking instead for some important documents, but she had no way of knowing where they might be stored. They might be in a locked desk drawer, a secure filing cabinet, or in a safe. We, as the author, know about the safe, and that sneaked into the way we wrote it. For Alexis, though, this would have been *a* safe, something she discovered in her hunt for the documents. If she returned to this room a second time, then it would become *the* safe.

I'll show you two contrasting examples so we can explore this a bit further.

> **Example 1:** Rob walked into the laboratory. A woman scientist leaned over a microscope at the far end.

> **Example 2:** Rob walked into a laboratory. The woman scientist leaned over a microscope at the far end.

In Example 1, Rob knew about the laboratory and intended to go there specifically. It might even be the only laboratory. When he enters, a woman he either doesn't know or doesn't immediately recognize is working at a microscope.

In Example 2, Rob hasn't been in this laboratory before. It might even be one of many. He might not have known it was a laboratory before he entered. We have quite a few options depending on our needs. When he enters, though, he discovers a woman he already knows at the microscope.

Because we've called her "the woman," however, we've also made it clear that Rob doesn't yet know her name even though he's seen her before. Maybe she's the only woman scientist he's seen or knows about in this building.

If he knew her name, we'd need to write this instead...

Rob walked into a laboratory. Melissa leaned over a micro-scope at the far end.

When we first start to write in deep POV, it can seem like a momentous shift in thinking. That's why I suggest thinking about it as if we literally were the viewpoint character. Any time we're in doubt about whether or not we've violated deep POV, we can run it through that filter and have our answer. Is the element we're questioning something we could experience were we in the identical situation? If not, away it goes.

A NOTE FOR FANTASY AND SCIENCE FICTION WRITERS

Some of you, like me, might write in a genre that can allow for mind-reading, emotion-reading, extra-sensory perception, precognition, or some other special ability that breaks one of these guidelines. Here's my suggestion if that's the case.

Break that guideline, but keep all the others and set new limits. I'm sure you've all heard that magic should cost something. It's not just magic that should have restrictions and a price. What are the broader implications of what you've changed?

In a society of telepaths, for example, how does that complicate relationships? Are thoughts now as regulated as actions? How can a character survive in a world where there's constant mental noise? Or does telepathy require a conscious decision and take energy, much like swimming rather than sinking in a pool?

As soon as you change one of these normal human limits, it has a ripple effect. You shouldn't change one of these without considering the consequences.

When we take away too many limits from our characters, we also run into problems with keeping the tension and conflict in our books high enough. Our readers want to see our characters struggle. Don't make something easier without also making something else harder.

CHAPTER FIVE

The Interior Life

O NE OF THE QUALITIES THAT DEFINES deep POV is placing the interior life of the viewpoint character on the page. We brushed up against this with the unbreakable rule of deep POV in the last chapter, but because there are multiple facets to the interior life, I'm going to dig into it in more detail in this chapter.

As I mentioned in Chapter One, the interior life includes visceral reactions, motivations, and internal dialogue (character thoughts).

VISCERAL REACTIONS

Visceral reactions are bodily responses we have no control over—dizziness, a racing heart, sweaty palms, tense shoulders, a clenched stomach, etc.

They're involuntary or instinctive, and they happen in reaction to a stimulus of either a thought or an event. While we can sometimes manage them once they happen, they initially come without our conscious decision or will.

These involuntary responses are also the expression of emotions. It's the way our body feels inside when we're gripped by hatred for the drunk driver who killed our friend. It's the rush of excitement or love. It's the paralyzing hit of fear. But instead of naming (i.e. telling) those emotions, visceral reactions allow us to show them to the reader.

These responses can be internal or external. They can be known only to the viewpoint character (a rolling stomach) or visible to all (shaking hands).

Visceral reactions are a hallmark of deep POV. They're part of what engages the reader and makes the reader feel along with the viewpoint character. So to write deep POV well, we need to understand visceral responses and when to use them.

Only visceral reactions by the viewpoint character count for building deep POV.

Deep POV is about the viewpoint character, so when I talk about visceral reactions, I mean those experienced by the viewpoint character. Those are the ones the reader will experience as if they were their own.

Visceral reactions by non-viewpoint characters will either be unknown or will show through external evidence, but they won't be felt by the reader in the same way. They're second-hand, filtered through the perspective of our viewpoint character and interpreted by them. Our viewpoint character can (and often should) respond to those signals, but their response is what matters most in that case.

Understanding the distinction between visceral reactions belonging to our viewpoint character and those belonging to non-viewpoint characters is important because we need to make sure we include visceral reactions by our viewpoint character. Sometimes, if we're having great physical responses by other characters, we can forget to include visceral reactions belonging to our viewpoint character as well.

Watch your frequency.

Think about visceral reactions as cayenne pepper. A dash adds a special bite to your dish. A scoop burns out your taste buds and ensures you won't want to eat that dish again. We want to use visceral reactions strategically, but we don't want to burn the reader out emotionally by overusing them. If you've ever read a book where the character's heart pounded so often you were worried they were about to have a heart attack, you know what I mean.

Exactly how often we use these emotional hits depends on our book and our writing style, but a good general guideline is to include a few per chapter. Sound too general to be helpful? I'll explain how you can know when might be the right time.

Think for a minute about when you've experienced an involuntary, visceral reaction in your life. Unless you're sick, these reactions didn't hit you without a cause. And that cause wasn't something mundane like "I need to add milk to the grocery list." It was something important to you.

Maybe someone said to you, "I have bad news." Maybe you remembered an appointment 10 minutes after you were supposed to be there. Maybe someone you love showed up at your door unexpectedly. Or maybe you heard a strange noise in the house at night when you're all alone.

Save the visceral reactions as responses to what matters and your reader will feel the emotions even more deeply.

Beware of interpreting them.

On rare occasions, it's alright to both show and tell, but this is the exception, not the norm. So when you're adding visceral reactions, make sure you give the evidence and stop.

Showing and Telling: Her hands shook with fear.

Just the Evidence (Showing): Her hands shook.

Readers are smart. They'll understand from the context why her hands were shaking.

Write fresh.

When we first start adding visceral reactions, it can be easy to default to phrases like "her heart pounded." That's alright once in a while, but our hearts can do more than pound, flutter, and race. Even if that's what our viewpoint character's heart is doing, we can still find creative ways to describe it. I'll give you a couple of quick examples.

Her heart punched against the bottom of her throat. – from *Cursed Wishes* by Marcy Kennedy

Her heart couldn't decide whether it was going to stop or beat a thousand times a second. – from *Pure Sacrifice* by Jami Gold

Don't repeat yourself.

In the first draft of my soon-to-be-released historical fantasy *Cursed Wishes*, I mentioned stomachs over 30 times. When I looked at these passages side-by-side it was easy to see patterns I'd fallen in to.

We don't need to worry about this during our first draft, but when it comes time to revise, the visceral reactions are spots where we need to spend a little extra time and creativity.

MOTIVATIONS FOR GOALS AND DECISIONS

One of the most common reasons writers struggle when creating deep POV stories has to do with failing to properly motivate our viewpoint character or with failing to reveal their motivation through internal dialogue.

Motivation is the reason (or reasons) *why* our character does what they do. It's the reason they want to reach their goal.

Because motivation is one of the keys to successfully writing in deep POV, allow me to explain it a bit more.

In stories written from a farther narrative distance, the reader won't always know why the protagonist acts the way he or she does. They'll sometimes have to guess based on what they see the character doing. That separation from the protagonist's driving motivation is part of what contributes to the feeling of distance. And distance is anathema in deep POV.

(Just so we're clear, regardless of the narrative distance in our stories, our characters always need proper motivation for their goals and decisions. The difference between deep POV stories and stories written from a farther narrative distance is how and how much of those motivations we share with the reader.)

Motivation also matters more in deep POV than in any other narrative distance because we're inside the character, experiencing the world through them. So a motivation that doesn't make sense or doesn't fit our character immediately destroys the story for the reader. They lose connection with the character, and they stop believing the story is possible.

To put this another way, the success of our deep POV story hinges on properly establishing and maintaining motivation for our viewpoint characters. When the motivations don't work, the story falls apart.

Motivation comes on two levels.

Our protagonist needs an overall story motivation.

What drives them to pursue their big-picture story goal? Why do they want that thing so badly that they'll suffer through the challenges the story throws at them?

I mentioned this already, but it bears repeating—the motivation we choose needs to match the character and be believable based on her personality and history.

For example, say we have a woman who wants to save the lives of cancer patients because she watched her mother suffer and die from brain cancer. Great. But now say that woman also faints at the sight of blood. If you set her off to be a neurosurgeon, you lose believability. If you set her off to be a cancer researcher, however, you've matched her goal and motivation to her personality and history.

The motivation also needs to be strong. Readers won't believe that a weak motivation would keep our character going through the trials that make a story interesting.

If our future cancer researcher doesn't have the money for a university education, the memory of her dead mother and her desire to spare others from that same pain will carry her through. The memory of watching a surgery on TV as a child and thinking it was cool won't. She'll quit and go find a different dream because her motivation isn't strong enough. If you make her keep going with that weak motivation, your reader won't believe that she'd actually soldier on in the way you're showing. Unless we're strongly motivated otherwise, we, as human beings, tend to take the easiest path.

Our protagonist also needs motivation for each step she takes and decision she makes along the way.

We can have our characters do almost anything in a story as long as we establish a strong motivation for it. We need to share with the reader why our viewpoint character makes each choice they make. Remember that a choice means they have more than one option and they're not reacting on instinct. If someone throws a punch, our character will instinctively duck. We don't need to share the motivation for that.

But if our character is being kidnapped by a man with a knife, she has a choice to make. Does she fight him? Or does she go along with whatever he tells her to do?

Which choice she makes depends on her motivation. Does she choose not to fight because she doesn't know how to defend herself and believes he'll kill her if she tries? Or does she choose to fight because she was a high school track star and knows if she can break free she can also outrun him?

As long as we understand and believe her reasons for whatever choice she makes, we'll go along with her actions. If we don't understand, you risk the reader thinking your character is stupid for not doing XYZ obvious thing. Let her think about XYZ obvious thing and dismiss it for a good reason instead. Motivation matters.

Like with visceral reactions, though, it's not enough to include them. We need to include them in the right way. *The right way* means we phrase the motivation in the way our character would think about it rather than stating it in a *telling* or *stating-a-fact* way.

I'll give you an example.

Telly Motivation Share: She wanted to get away from him.

Improved Motivation Share:

The hand he placed on her arm grew in weight until her knees wobbled from the pressure of bearing it.

She glanced backward. No one stood between her and the door. She could tell him she'd forgotten an appointment. Or she wasn't feeling well. Or that she still lived with her father and he demanded she be home by 8:00 pm every night.

Any lie or level of embarrassment would be better than continuing to stand here.

In the character-based example, you still understand her motivation, but it comes across in a way that's authentic to the character rather than in a way that feels like the author is just stating it.

CHARACTER THOUGHTS

Character thoughts in fiction go by many different names—internalizations, internal dialogue, internal monologue, interior monologue, inner monologue, interior dialogue, and inner dialogue. Don't get caught up in the terminology. It's all just the character thinking.

This topic is big enough that I'd need a book in itself to cover it fully, but we need to look at it at least a bit here as it relates to deep POV and developing the internal life of our viewpoint character.

Thoughts need to be written in the viewpoint character's voice.

Remember that in deep POV, our author voice isn't on display. The story is shared in the voice and personality of the viewpoint character. One viewpoint character might see a five foot, 200 pound woman and think of the health risks she's facing because she's overweight. A character who's more of a jerk might insultingly think about her as a fat cow with no self-control. Just because we wouldn't phrase it that way doesn't mean our character wouldn't. The words on the page belong to them. It's their personality, not ours.

Only share thoughts that advance the story.

Because deep POV uses more internal dialogue than do stories written from a distant POV, we run the risk of becoming too lenient about what we include in internal dialogue. In fiction, everything needs a reason to be on the page. Each line of internal dialogue we include should reveal character, move the plot forward, or enhance subtler elements like the theme.

Share thoughts when the character would naturally think them.

Even a thought that advances the story will feel wrong if we include it in a place when the character wouldn't naturally be thinking it. Remember our rule about becoming the viewpoint character? If we're not sure whether this is the right moment for our character to think about something, we can ask ourselves what we'd be thinking in a similar situation. That's still a bit vague, though, because we're not our character. So I'll give you a few more guidelines about how to time internal dialogue.

Context

Context is everything when it comes to character thoughts.

If he's in a battle for his life, he won't be thinking about the origin of his sword or the fine etchings on the blade. If she's running through a museum after closing, being chased by a serial killer, she won't be noticing the art and artifacts around her (unless they'd make a great defensive weapon).

What a character thinks about and how much time they spend thinking about it depends on what else is happening to them at the same time.

Context also determines how they interpret what they see. A character in the woods might see a cave. If they're out for a leisurely hike, they'd worry about whether it was a bear den. If they're running for their life, they'd consider it as a hiding place and may not even think about the possibility of a bear until it's too late.

Reaction Basis

Internal dialogue needs to be a reaction to what came before it, whether the stimulus is something happening around our viewpoint character, a previous thought, or a visceral response. This has two sides. We need to check that our viewpoint character's thoughts connect in some way to what happened before them. We also need to make sure our viewpoint character reacts to important events through internal dialogue. For example, if we reveal a shocking piece of information—like an affair—our POV character better try to come to grips with it and think it through. You would, wouldn't you? If they don't have an appropriate reaction, the reader will feel like the story isn't believable.

External Triggers

Above I mentioned that internal dialogue can be a reaction to external triggers. I could have lumped external triggers in with *reaction basis*, but I didn't want to risk anyone overlooking the importance of external triggers themselves. External triggers help us solve the problems that come with backstory insertion and describing things that our viewpoint character normally wouldn't notice or comment on because they're so familiar with them.

Understanding that internal dialogue should be a reaction to an external trigger means that we're less likely to inappropriately drop in backstory when we're trying to write a deep POV story.

Here's what I mean by that. Backstory is challenging for us as writers because we tend to either include too much of it, slowing the story down, or drop it in when we—the author—want to tell the reader something, hence creating author intrusion and violating deep POV.

But in deep POV, backstory is nothing more than the viewpoint character thinking about an event that happened in their past.

Because of that, we'll know when to insert backstory because we'll insert it as an internal reaction by the viewpoint character to something else that happened. If there's no cause, no trigger, then it doesn't belong there. Backstory should always come as a reaction to a stimulus.

And we won't include too much backstory when we understand it as an internal dialogue reaction to something else that happened. When something triggers a memory for you, do you usually stop in the middle of what you're doing to think about it for five or ten minutes? No? Neither should our characters. Memories, thoughts of our past, pass quickly through our heads and cause another reaction. They cause us to either feel something or do something else.

Next to misplaced backstory, one of the most common errors I see in my work as an editor is when an author includes details that their viewpoint character never would have noticed because those details are commonplace to them. This violates deep POV. If they don't notice it and wouldn't think about it, we can't put it on the page.

The trick to solving this is "thoughts are a reaction to a trigger." If we want our viewpoint character to think about something they normally wouldn't pay attention to, we can give them a reason to think about that detail.

For example, say we have a character who collects priceless antiques. It breaks deep POV if we have them walk into their apartment and muse on their collection in detail. They see those items every day. There's no reason for them to stop on this day and think about them.

But if they come in and their Persian cat knocks over a priceless vase that our character catches a moment before it smashes on the floor—now they have a reason to think about the irreplaceable vase.

If you'd like to learn more about internal dialogue (a.k.a. character thoughts), take a look at my book *Internal Dialogue: A Busy Writer's Guide*.

BALANCING THE INTERIOR WORLD WITH THE EXTERIOR WORLD

Before I close out this chapter on the interior life of our viewpoint character, we need to quickly cover how to ensure we're not overdoing it on the interior. Deep POV critics often accuse deep POV of being too claustrophobic and prone to talking-head syndrome. Talking head syndrome is when we spend so much time focused on what's happening inside the character that it begins to feel like the character is in a bubble, separated from anything external.

The interior life is essential to building reader connection with our character, but too much of it can cost us reader connection with our story world. Good deep POV finds the balance between the internal and the external.

The way to balance the two isn't as complicated as it can seem at first. (I discuss this topic in even more depth as it relates to character thoughts in *Internal Dialogue* if you're interested in digging deeper into the topic. In this book, I'm only covering the part of it you need to know to write deep POV well.)

To find the balance, we alternate between paragraphs focused on the viewpoint character and paragraphs focused elsewhere. It might sound obvious or overly simplistic when I put it that way, but many writers don't do this and don't know they should be doing it.

So let me explain the two types of paragraphs, and we'll go forward from there.

A paragraph focusing on the viewpoint character can include that character acting, speaking, thinking, or feeling. Much of it will be things (like internal dialogue and emotion) that only the point-of-view character is aware of.

A paragraph that doesn't focus on the point-of-view character will include action done by other characters or action in the environment, dialogue spoken by other characters, or description of the setting or of other characters. These are elements that any character in the scene could experience and be aware of. It's public.

We need to alternate between the two. If we have a character-focused paragraph or two, then we need to make sure we switch to an external paragraph.

As a general guideline, we shouldn't combine the two. Each paragraph we write should be focused on one or the other.

The internal life connects closely with interpretation, so that's what we're going to look at next.

CHAPTER SIX

Interpretation

I N DEEP POV, EVERYTHING IS SUBJECTIVE. We're not presenting a factual, objective view of the world—and that's a good thing. A completely unbiased representation would be flat and uninteresting.

The challenge for us because of this is twofold. We need to write a subjective view of the story world. We also need to make sure that we're presenting the subjective view belonging to the viewpoint character.

We see the world tinted by our own history, personality, interests, and agendas. Often, we're not even aware of how our perception is biased. We make assumptions about the world, and we write based on those assumptions.

In deep POV, we need to try to set aside our views and replace them with the views of our viewpoint character. They're not us. They won't and shouldn't experience the world in the exact way we would. Yes, we're both sentient beings (I almost wrote "human beings" but some of us are science fiction and fantasy writers with nonhuman characters!), so we share the commonalities I talked about in the previous chapters.

But within that common framework, we're still individuals. We can't have our character working through our perception. It's not about what we would notice or how we would interpret the scene. It's about the viewpoint character's perception and interpretation.

Exploring the world from the perspective of someone else is an experience we can only have through fiction, and it's part of what makes reading such a fulfilling and interesting activity.

In this chapter, we're going to look at developing the subjective perception of the world required by deep POV.

DESCRIPTION SHOULD NEVER BE NEUTRAL

One of the biggest mistakes we can make in our writing is to use neutral, generic descriptions. This mistake is why so many writers wrongly believe that description is boring. Description, done right, is a vibrant, essential part of our story.

Description done right is filtered through the mind and senses of a viewpoint character. Coloring our descriptions with our viewpoint character's opinions brings them to life, enhances voice, and gives readers the exciting experience of seeing the world through someone else's eyes.

So how are some ways we can improve our deep POV using description?

Describe other characters based on how our viewpoint character feels about them.

If our viewpoint character is jealous of someone else, they'll focus on the flaws in that person's appearance. If our viewpoint character loves or admires someone, that will also influence the words they use to describe them and what they notice about them.

Even strangers aren't neutral because our viewpoint character will make assumptions about them based on their appearance and our viewpoint character's personality.

For example, is the biker on the street corner someone to be feared, criticized, or used as a source for the best bike shops and tattoo parlors? Our viewpoint character's opinion about bikers will in turn stretch out to influence what our viewpoint character describes about them and the word choices they make.

Describe setting based on the emotions of the viewpoint character and their personality.

Does that café our protagonist visited for lunch have character, or is it grungy and run-down? That depends on who our viewpoint character is and how they're feeling that day.

For example, if our viewpoint character has just lost their job, they're more likely to see the cracked tiles on the floor and the flickering overhead lighting. If they're meeting up with their new love interest, though, and they're excited and happy, the same lighting adds ambiance and they'll notice the quirky paintings on the walls.

I'll give you an example of character personality influencing what's noticed before I move on. This time I'll actually show it. Two different characters are entering the same hospital emergency room.

Character 1:

> Carol pushed open the door and strode into the emergency room waiting area. Clean floors, bright lighting, seats clearly selected with patient comfort in mind. She glanced back over her shoulder. They could use an automatic revolving door to better serve patients with disabilities, but other

than that, she really couldn't find much to criticize. She'd always believed in first impressions, and her first impression told her she'd like working here.

Character 2:

Katie tugged her sleeve over her hand and nudged open the emergency room door with her covered fist. With so many sick people going in and out, an automatic door would have made more sense. She stopped just inside. In the middle of the room, a man hunched over and barked a cough into his hands, and on the far end, a girl with a red face—probably a fever—squirmed in her mother's lap. With the chairs so few in number and close together, there'd be no way to avoid either of their germs if she actually sat down. Maybe she could just stand in the corner until her turn came.

Carol is likely a nurse or a doctor. She's not worried about being around sick people. What she notices is how well-maintained the hospital appears because that's going to affect her work-life satisfaction.

Katie, on the other hand, is a patient who's uncomfortable in a hospital setting. She doesn't care about the lighting or the ergonomic chairs. What she focuses on are the other sick people, disease carriers who might infect her.

Both women noticed the manual door, but why it bothered them was also influenced by their personalities. Helper Carol sees how the patient situation could be improved. Hypochondriac Katie sees another way she might contract something.

Keep in mind occupation, hobbies, and past history when describing a situation.

A Catholic priest, a home inspector, and an amateur chef all walk into the same kitchen. (No, that's not the start of a bad joke.) What they notice will differ.

The Catholic priest will notice the crucifix on the wall and the well-worn Bible on the kitchen table. The home inspector will notice the cracked plaster in the ceiling and the touch of mold starting on the base boards. The chef will notice the beautiful set of knives and the herbs hung to dry in the window.

Or they could notice the lack of those items. What we choose to show depends on both the viewpoint character and on the impression we want to give of the place where they are and the people who live or work there.

I'll give you another example.

Boring, generic description: Tall trees lined the path.

Description from the eyes of a horticulturalist: Silver birch trees lined the path. Their tall white trunks reached straight and healthy, but chunks were missing from their leaves. The sawfly larvae were feasting again.

Description from the eyes of someone with allergies: Sunlight filtered down through the trees' raggedy leaves, illuminating every particle of pollen and dust floating in the air. She sneezed and hurried forward, pressure already building in her sinuses.

In life, everything we experience is influenced by who we are. It should be the same when we're writing in deep POV.

Use similes and metaphors that fit the character.

A simile is a figure of speech that compares two unlike things that resemble each other in some way, often using the words *like* or *as*.

> The strangely shaped fruit tasted like strawberries and citrus.

The flavor of the fruit resembles other flavors that the character is familiar with. Similes help bring descriptions to life by relating the unknown to the known.

A metaphor is a figure of speech that says something is something else.

> All the world's a stage,
> And all the men and women merely players
> – William Shakespeare, *As You Like It*, Act II, Scene VII

> The house was a refrigerator.

We know that the world isn't literally a stage and that the people in it aren't literally all actors. We also know the house wasn't literally a fridge. But in some ways, some important ways, they are the same. Metaphors add depth to writing.

When we're looking at similes and metaphors in deep POV, we need to build these comparisons using items our viewpoint character is familiar with.

In my short story "A Purple Elephant," in my ebook *Frozen*, my viewpoint character is a chef. So when she wakes up in the hospital after a near-death experience, here's how she describes the way she's feeling:

I was in a hospital bed when I regained consciousness. An IV needled poked from the delicate skin on the back of my hand, and I felt like a piece of raw meat pounded flat.

In another work-in-progress, I have a science teacher. When she's embarrassed, here's how she describes it:

> Her face smoldered as if she'd bent too close over one of the Bunsen burners used in her class.

We don't need to make each figure of speech job-specific, but they should all be tailored to the character. A character who's never set foot on a boat won't think something like the following when she's trapped in an earthquake:

> The ground beneath her rolled and bucked like a ship on stormy water.

That's not in her frame of reference. Our minds make comparisons with things we know well. It doesn't matter how great the figure of speech is. If it doesn't fit our character, we shouldn't use it.

If that character enjoyed amusement parks, she might think about the earthquake this way instead:

> The ground beneath her plunged and rolled, leaving her feeling like she was riding a rollercoaster standing up.

But similes and metaphors in deep POV aren't just about what our viewpoint character knows and is familiar with. We can also use them to imply their personality and perspective. I'll show you two examples.

> He pulled his hand away from the knife wound in his belly and reach toward me, oozing liquid onto the floor like a gutted deer strung up to bleed out.

He pulled his hand away from the knife wound in his belly and reached toward me, blood dripping from his fingers like tears.

The character who would think the first is very different from the character who would think the second.

PAY ATTENTION TO HOW YOUR VIEWPOINT CHARACTER NAMES PEOPLE AND ITEMS

At first this might look like a strange point to include in a chapter on interpretation, but this is a common mistake writers make both when writing in deep POV and in other narrative depths.

When naming people or things, we should be consistent rather than trying to add variety to the names. We think about the people we know in one specific way. I play the flute at my church, and the other woman I play with is named Tina. I only ever think of Tina as Tina. I don't think about her as *the other flutist* or as *Mrs. G.*

Yet, when we write, within the same scene we might have our viewpoint character think about someone as Michael, the young construction worker, and the man. We don't do that in real life. We've violated deep POV.

We do sometimes change how we speak about someone, but that's because we're catering to the person we're speaking to. I call my husband *Chris* when I'm speaking to him or to someone who knows him. When I talk to someone who doesn't know him, I call him *my husband*. How I personally think about him in my mind, however, stays the same. So when writers change the way their viewpoint character thinks about someone, they're unintentionally violating deep POV. Our character has no audience to their thoughts, and so they'll think about each person and each object in only one way.

The exception to this is if we're using the removal or change of a name to indicate a change in the relationship. Remember, how our viewpoint character sees the world is subjective.

Say, for example, that we have a man named James who meets a woman scientist named Dr. Megan Hargrove. Perhaps when they met and were introduced, Dr. Megan Hargrove was rude or abrupt with him. He might strip her of her name in his thoughts to create emotional distance from someone he has an adversarial relationship with. As that relationship changes, so will the way he thinks about her.

The important thing to remember is that this switch will be deliberate, and will show clear progress rather than swapping back and forth randomly. She might start out as "that woman scientist," progress to "Dr. Hargrove," and end up as "Megan."

Names matter and they carry power. You can see another good example of this in the Harry Potter books. Voldemort starts out as He-Who-Must-Not-Be-Named because he's feared. As the series progresses and rebellion and courage build, the characters start referring to him as Voldemort or even by his muggle name of Tom Riddle.

CREATE A SENSE OF INTERNAL JUDGMENT BY USING EVIDENTIAL ADVERBS AND MODAL VERBS

I'm not a fan of trying to make writers memorize a lot of grammatical terms. So I'll quickly explain what evidential adverbs and modal verbs are, and then, once you understand the concept, you're welcome to forget the technical terms for them.

An adverb is a word that modifies a verb (an action word) or a clause. An evidential adverb is one which expresses certainty or uncertainty. Examples include *apparently, obviously, of course, clearly, surely, no doubt, naturally,* and *likely.*

Modal verbs are words used to indicate likelihood, permission, obligation, or ability. Examples include *can, could, may, might, must, shall, should, will,* and *would.*

Back in the chapter on Limited Knowledge, I pointed out that one of the ways to avoid point-of-view errors and violating deep POV is to make it clear that our viewpoint character is interpreting the situation. Evidential adverbs and modal verbs help us do that. Using these creates the sense that our viewpoint character has to interpret what's happening around them rather than that some omniscient narrator is dictating black-and-white facts.

I'll show you an example. This first sentence feels like the author dictating a fact.

He was still angry at her for getting the promotion instead of him.

In this second sentence, adding an evidential adverb makes it clear that this is the viewpoint character's interpretation of the situation.

No doubt he was still angry at her for getting the promotion instead of him.

Evidential adverbs and modal verbs are essential to deep POV because one of the fascinating and fun elements of deep POV is that our viewpoint character will make assumptions, they'll have biased or unfounded opinions, they'll be confused, and they'll be proven wrong later in the story.

We do need to watch out for one potential pitfall when using them, though. We should use them when there's some room for interpretation by the viewpoint character or when they are making an assumption or guess. We shouldn't use them when what they're commenting on is what it is.

I'll italicize and underline the problem word in the example I'm going to show you.

Problematic: Angie _seemed_ sad, red ringing her eyes and her shoulders sagging forward like she wanted to make herself disappear.

By all evidence, Angie actually does seem sad. So now we have a confused reader. Does the viewpoint character think for some reason that Angie isn't sad? There's nothing to indicate that's the case except for the word _seemed_.

If Angie actually is sad, then we shouldn't use _seemed_. (In fact, if Angie really is sad, we shouldn't tell the reader she's sad at all. We should just show them the evidence.)

If the viewpoint character suspects she really isn't sad, then we need to show why they're making that assumption.

Fixed: Angie seemed sad, but she'd always been a good actor. She was probably dancing inside over the pile of money she'd inherit now that Grant was gone.

See the difference? If our viewpoint character believes something to be fact, then we have to be careful about introducing words that unintentionally introduce doubt.

Appeared and _looked_ can cause us the same problems as _seemed_.

Make sure when you use these words that there's room for interpretation in what your viewpoint character sees. They should be used only when what's in front of them might not be what it appears, seems, or looks to be.

CHAPTER SEVEN

An Inside-Out Perspective

DEEP POV IS ALL ABOUT TRYING TO SHARE a story in such a way that the reader feels like they are the character or that they're being carried along inside the character. One way you can think about it is that it's like trying to make the reader a ghost inhabiting the body of the character. The character isn't aware of them, but the ghost experiences everything along with them, living vicariously through them.

That approach requires a perspective shift to viewing the world from the inside-out. The way we experience our own life is different from how we experience the lives of people who are separate from us.

We see their lives from the outside. We look at them.

We see our lives from the inside. We're looking out at the world. We're not looking at ourselves.

In this chapter, I'm going to show you the most important items to watch for when you're trying to write from the inside-out.

CHECK YOUR "CAMERA" ANGLE

We can also think about this as the eye of the narrator. Where does it feel like the narrator is sitting? It should feel like they're inside the viewpoint character's body.

I'll give you a few examples. Let's say our viewpoint character is Andrea.

Outside-In Perspective: Andrea's face turned red.

Andrea can't see her own face. This is from the perspective of someone looking at Andrea, but if we *are* Andrea, we don't experience it this way.

Inside-Out Perspective: Heat burned up her neck and into her cheeks.

If we're Andrea, we experience it from the inside—what we feel.

I'll show you one more example so you can see the difference—it's subtle but important.

Outside-In Perspective: A smirk spread across Andrea's lips.

Again, Andrea can't see her own face. This feels like it's coming from the perspective of someone watching Andrea from the outside. Andrea experiences this differently.

Inside-Out Perspective: Andrea smirked.

Her smirking is an action that she does. We're now inside Andrea, participating in the action, rather than outside Andrea, watching her act.

The camera angle can be a bit tricky to manage initially because there's no shortcut for catching the errors the way there are for some of the other points in this chapter. However, the most likely area to make a camera-angle mistake is in the viewpoint character's face. This tends to happen because we're often imagining what our character looks like as we write instead of trying to slip into their skin and imagine what they're feeling.

Watch for changes in skin tone.

The most likely culprits are paling, redness, blueness (especially around the lips), or green tinges.

Watch for spots where you might have described an expression rather than having the character act.

The lips are usually where the major problems show up with smiles, smirks, frowns, thinned lips, etc. The eyes can also cause us troubles, though. For example, *her eyes narrowed* vs. *she narrowed her eyes*. I'll talk about this a bit more when we look at body parts moving on their own.

Watch for facial tics your viewpoint character might not notice.

This ties in to what we talked about earlier in the chapter on limited knowledge. A muscle jumping in a character's cheek, a twitch in their eye, and other minor facial cues might or might not be noticed by the viewpoint character themselves. We have to be very careful about including them and about how we describe them. The fewer facial tics we include from the viewpoint character, the better, and when we do mention them, we need to justify it.

If our viewpoint character notices her eye twitching, for example, it will probably be coupled with an emotion of frustration or with covering her eye to try to make it stop. That's an inside-out perspective. It won't likely be a simple mention like *a muscle in her eye twitched* because that feels like it's coming from the perspective of someone outside, watching her. Unless it's bothering her or she has an opinion on that twitching muscle, she won't comment on it in herself.

A twitch in someone else's eye, however, might be noticed by the viewpoint character as a clue that they're lying or nervous or need more sleep. We're much more likely to notice facial tics in other people than we are to notice them in ourselves. If they're habitual tics in our own face, we'll never notice them.

ELIMINATE FILTERING WORDS AND PHRASES THAT CREATE NARRATIVE DISTANCE

The problem with filtering words when we're writing in deep POV is that they make it feel like someone else is telling us about the character (observing them from the outside) rather than like we're living the experience through the character (from the inside).

Filtering words fall into a couple categories, but the principle behind them is the same so I'm going to cover them together.

The five senses words—*felt, heard, tasted, saw,* and *smelled.*

With Distance: Gabby heard a floorboard creak behind her and she froze.

In Deep POV: A floorboard behind her creaked. Gabby froze.

When we're in deep POV, we have a single viewpoint character. What that means is that we can only describe what that viewpoint character experiences. So saying "Gabby heard" something is unnecessarily wordy and redundant. If Gabby didn't hear it, we couldn't include it.

Beyond this, how often do we think about the fact that we saw or smelled something? We don't think...

I see my dog running loose on the road.

We think something like...

Crap! The dog's loose on the road again.

As soon as we add one of the five senses words, we've come out of deep POV and we've added a layer of distance.

Thought words and thought tags—*thought, knew, wondered, realized, wished, decided, remembered, recalled,* etc.

With Distance: Jessica stopped in the middle of the zoo food court and stared at the cheerfully revolving carousel. She thought about the times they used to ride the carousel together. She swallowed down the lump in her throat and turned away.

In Deep POV: Jessica stopped in the middle of the zoo food court. In front of her, a carousel revolved cheerfully, a mish-mash of bright colors. They used to ride the carousel together, back when Dad still lived with them. A lump formed in her throat. She swallowed it down and turned away. She was too big for carousel rides anymore anyway.

Obviously, I've fleshed out the deep POV example, but that's because the changes we make when writing in deep POV won't be a one-for-one word swap with more distant writing. That's okay. Tight, powerful writing has less to do with the number of words used and more to do with making every word count.

These "thinking" words add distance for the same reasons as the "sensing" words add distance. Since we're in the viewpoint character's mind, anything we include must be something they're thinking about. If they're not thinking about it, we can't include it.

It also adds distance because, in the same way that we don't think about the fact that we're sensing something, we also don't consciously think about thinking. We don't think...

I'm wondering if he's going to stand me up.

Or...

I just decided I'm going on a diet tomorrow.

That's how we might say those things out loud, but when we're thinking, we simply think the content.

Is he going to stand me up?

I'm going on a diet tomorrow.

If you read my internal dialogue book, you'll see that this is one of the reasons I advise against using tags like *he thought* when we're writing in third-person point of view. It holds the reader an additional step back from the viewpoint character and makes it feel like someone else, not the character, is telling them what's happening. Instead, in deep POV, we want the immediacy of showing the reader what's happening with no distance between them and the viewpoint character. (More on immediacy in the next chapter!)

A hint to help us spot these filtering words is to look for the use of personal pronouns (*he/she/I*) during descriptions (when your character perceives something and it's conveyed to the reader) or when your viewpoint character is judging or evaluating something (a.k.a. when they're thinking).

REDUCE YOUR DIALOGUE TAGS TO THE BARE MINIMUM

Dialogue tags used correctly are a good and useful tool. Sometimes they're necessary to maintain forward momentum without losing clarity. (If you're not sure how to use them correctly, I suggest you check out my book *Dialogue: A Busy Writer's Guide*.)

However, dialogue tags also add a bit of distance. Say we had a sentence like this.

"I don't want to go out tonight," she said.

If our viewpoint character is the *she* in the tag, then technically she wouldn't be thinking *she said* after she speaks.

If our viewpoint character is another character, then technically our viewpoint character also wouldn't be thinking *she said* after the other woman speaks.

In both cases, the viewpoint character would simply hear or speak the words.

We can't always avoid dialogue tags. What we can do is try to minimize them by using action beats instead. In that case, our sentence above might become something like this.

She slid her feet into the pair of pink fuzzy slippers she always kept near the bed. "I don't want to go out tonight."

The danger here is that we start adding empty action that can slow down the pace of our writing. The solution isn't to simply sub in dialogue tags or to leave our dialogue tagless when that risks confusing the reader. The solution is to make sure that every piece of description and action we use serves a bigger purpose by setting the mood, adding subtext, etc.

(If you'd like to know when my book *Description* releases, please sign up for my newsletter.)

USE YOUR VIEWPOINT CHARACTER'S NAME LESS IN THEIR VIEWPOINT SCENES

The more we use our viewpoint character's name in their own scenes, the greater the distance we create from that character. As a general guideline, we should try to use their name only when necessary to provide clarity. The rest of the time we should stick to *he* or *she*.

And make sure that you don't swap up what they're called. If our viewpoint character is named Rebecca, we can call her *Rebecca* or *she*, but we shouldn't also refer to her as *the young teacher* or *the woman*. She wouldn't be thinking about herself that way anymore than she would swap up the way she thinks about someone else.

DON'T NAME EMOTIONS

Writing concepts are often much like different colored strands within the same tapestry. They're each unique from the others, and yet, they're all interconnected. Writing in deep POV and showing rather than telling in particular share a lot of the same DNA. Naming emotions causes problems for both deep POV and for showing.

(If you don't know what I mean by *showing rather than telling,* please read Appendix B before continuing with this section. I'm not going to cover showing vs. telling in depth here because it's not the topic of this book.)

Whenever we give a label to what our character is feeling—whether it be a viewpoint character or not—we're telling rather than showing.

He was angry. She felt guilty. He hated her.

This labeling can also sneak into our dialogue tags.

"He's gone," she said sadly.

Telling emotions keeps the reader at arm's length rather than letting them experience the emotions along with the character. Remember, in deep POV, we want to experience the emotions as the character experiences them. Told emotions feel secondhand.

When we're talking about deep POV, this also becomes about the fact that, when we simply label an emotion, we don't really know how this feels to the character specifically, and it's too self-aware.

Most emotions in life are nuanced. Telling allows you to convey only the most basic part of the emotion, whereas showing allows you to bring out all the facets. In deep POV, we need the facets because that's part of what makes those emotions genuine and believable and individual to the character while still being relatable for the reader.

Take the example of Miriam, whose husband cheated on her. What's Miriam feeling?

Anger of course, you say. She probably is angry, but anger is usually a shield for other emotions. If we simply tell the reader she's angry, we miss the layers.

Is her anger motivated by fear that he's going to leave her? Wounded pride and self-esteem because she wasn't enough for him? Jealousy because he spent time with this other woman when their son needed him?

On the other hand, Miriam could be feeling relief because she's wanted to divorce her husband for years and now she has an excuse. Or because she cheated on him as well. Her anger is only a cover. She'll get more in the divorce that way.

Just maybe, Miriam is secretly happy that her husband cheated. He's always pretended to be so perfect, telling her how lucky she is that he puts up with her, making her feel like an inconvenience, like the rock stuck in the tread of his shoe. Now she has proof that other people won't be able to ignore. Yet she can't let them know she's happy. She'd lose the sympathy she craves if she did that.

The nuance of how this particular character experiences that emotion matters.

Naming emotions is also particularly problematic in deep POV because of how self-aware it is. Most of us don't stop while in the throes of an emotion to define what we're feeling. We're too busy feeling angry to stop and think, "I'm angry."

So how do we convey emotions without naming them? We can use physical reactions (usually internal or external instinctive reactions that can't be controlled), internal dialogue, and action. We can use dialogue for this as well, but dialogue can't always be believably substituted for what's happening inside or an emotion that needs a physical expression.

Sometimes we're afraid that, if we don't name the emotions, the reader won't clearly understand what we mean. The solution to that isn't to name the emotion. The solution is to make sure that the surrounding context makes it clear.

REMEMBER THAT YOUR CHARACTER IS THE CENTER OF THEIR OWN UNIVERSE

No one likes a narcissist (except the narcissist themselves), but we are all the heroes of our own story. We think about the world in relation to ourselves. So when we're writing deep POV, we have to remember that our viewpoint character is at the center. We, as the authors, are not.

This can come in the form of pointing words such as *here/there* and *this/that*. Wherever our viewpoint character is located will be *here* to them. Spots where they are not will be *there*.

The same is true for *this* and *that*. We want *this* one, not *that* one. Which becomes *this* and which becomes *that* depends on our viewpoint character's position and desire.

We'll normally get these right because they're more natural, but not always. Let's create a viewpoint character named Frank for this example.

> Frank tore the eviction notice off the door and crumpled it into a ball. He'd lived there for twenty years. No way was he moving now, new highway or no new highway.

This is mostly okay except for the use of *there*. While it's not technically wrong, it feels more distant because, to Frank, the spot in which he's standing, the spot in which he's living, is *here*. It's not a *there*.

Swapping *here* for *there* adds an additional subtle layer of closeness, which is what we're trying to create in deep POV.

> Frank tore the eviction notice off the door and crumpled it into a ball. He'd lived here for twenty years. No way was he moving now, new highway or no new highway.

Who is at the center should also be reflected in the way people are referenced. I've already covered this in depth in previous points and chapters, so I'll just touch on it briefly again here. If John is our viewpoint character, which of the following would be correct?

> **Option A:** John's wife handed him the paper and pointed at the front-page headline.

> **Option B:** His wife handed him the paper and pointed at the front-page headline.

> **Option C:** Lynn handed him the paper and pointed at the front-page headline.

Option C is correct because, to him, she's Lynn. He's not going to think about her by her title. The title feels like someone on the outside is commenting on their relationship status and pointing it out to an observer. It feels that way because we only reference someone by their relationship to us when we're explaining that relationship to an outsider.

The most common way we tend to violate the center in deep POV, though, is when we're referencing time. When we're thinking about time in relation to us, we think about *last night, yesterday, tomorrow*. We don't think about *the night before, the day before*, or *the next day*. Those are external labels for time that views the time from on high and outside of it. When they slip into our writing, they make it feel like someone outside the viewpoint character is defining the time rather than the character doing so themselves.

ELIMINATE BODY PARTS MOVING ON THEIR OWN

We want to avoid independently moving body parts for more reasons than just perspective. These types of sentences can be unintentionally funny to the reader.

Her eyes darted across the room.

How is she going to see without her eyes?

Their eyes connected.

Are they going to be able to disconnect them later?

Her eyes fell to her plate.

Umm, ouch.

Some readers might know what you mean, but others won't. And even if a reader figures it out, this breaks the fictional dream, however briefly. That's true regardless of whether the rogue body parts belong to a viewpoint character or a non-viewpoint character.

Aside from being unintentionally funny or creating strange and awkward word pictures in the reader's mind, body parts that move on their own shift the focus. Body parts that move independently take the character out of the equation. When readers have trouble connecting to the characters in a story, this can sometimes be the cause because we've removed the characters from the central role they should be playing.

From the point of view of writing in deep POV, animating body parts in this way makes it feel like we're outside the character again. We see the body parts acting. The character doesn't seem to have any part in it.

For example...

Her hand shot up.

It really didn't. She chose, at least on an instinctive level, to put her hand up. Her hand did not act alone (unless she really is possessed).

Fixed: She shot her hand into the air.

One more example.

Rogue Body Part: His fist pounded on the door.

His fist does not act outside of his will. He's the one pounding on the door. He uses his fist to do it.

Fixed: He pounded on the door.

Are there exceptions to this? Of course. If you've ever heard me teach, then you know I emphasize guidelines rather than rules. Guidelines are best practices that will yield the best possible result most of the time. Rules should never be broken. This is a guideline, not a rule.

In this case, we might want to violate this guideline if we're writing something intentionally metaphoric or if we need to add special emphasis to the body part itself.

For example, we might have a situation where one character can't act true to his desires. He hates what he has to do and wishes it could be different, but saying so openly would put his life in jeopardy or cause some other negative repercussion. We might write something like the following.

His eyes pled with her to forgive him.

We might also have a situation where we want to create the impression that the character is disconnected or that one part of them is in disagreement with the other part.

For example, say someone has come to our viewpoint character to show her evidence that her husband is cheating on her. Some part of her will want to know the truth. Another part will want to protect the life she has because she's happy. In that case, we might write...

> I drew back in my seat, away from the offered envelope, but my hand reached for it anyway.

The important thing to remember is that these are exceptions. We'll break the guideline occasionally for special effect. Regular use of independently moving body parts hurts our writing by disrupting deep POV, being unintentionally funny, and disconnecting readers from the characters.

CHAPTER EIGHT

Immediacy

IMMEDIACY MEANS THAT WE'RE experiencing the story in "real time." When we're reading, the events play out in front of us as if we were watching them at the same time as they're happening.

Think about the way you experience a TV show or movie. There's a sense that we're somehow watching the events at the time that they're taking place, like we're a high-tech spying device or the proverbial fly on the wall. We don't have the sense of a time lapse between when things happened and when we're hearing about them.

We can recreate this "real time" feeling in fiction, and in deep POV, that's exactly what we want to do. In Chapter One, I said this isn't a matter of tense. Even in past tense, this should be what we're striving for.

So in this chapter, that's exactly what we're going to be looking at.

MAINTAIN THE CORRECT CAUSE-AND-EFFECT ORDER

To write with immediacy, we must write linearly. We're inside our viewpoint character as things are happening, and that means they have to be on the page in the correct order.

To put this another way, we have to make sure that our cause comes before our effect. An action must come before the reaction to that action. This is how the world naturally works. It's the way it needs to work in our fiction if we're writing in deep POV or want to show rather than tell. (Setting aside those of you who might be writing a novel with a temporal paradox, of course.)

Unfortunately, we can easily reverse our cause and effect unintentionally for many reasons. Perhaps we're trying to add variety to our sentences and we don't think about what we're accidentally doing. Perhaps we just didn't realize it was a problem.

When you reverse the two so that the effect comes first, your readers will feel thrown off-balance and disconnected from your writing, even if they can't always tell you why. Because of that, we want to maintain the proper cause-and-effect order no matter what depth we're writing at, but when we write in deep POV, it becomes essential. Violating cause and effect destroys immediacy and adds distance.

The easiest way to spot cause and effect problems is to look for the words *as*, *while*, and *when*.

They're often used as connections between things that are supposed to be happening at the same time. Often, they're not actually happening at the same time. Often, you're messing up your cause and effect.

Let me give you an example of what I mean.

As the shot rang out, Ellen covered her ears.

No, she didn't. Not unless she's psychic. She couldn't have done what the sentence says because, until she heard the shot, Ellen had no reason to cover her ears.

The shot rang out, and Ellen covered her ears.

Let me give you a look at another way this could appear.

He blushed as he realized his fly was undone.

Blushing is the result or effect of realizing his fly is undone. This sentence feels odd because the cause and effect are flipped. He realizes his fly is undone, and as a result, his face heats. (*Realized* is a dangerous word in our fiction for other reasons as well, but we've already looked at those reasons so I won't repeat them here.)

I'll give you another example, using *when* instead.

We dove behind the couch when we heard our dad stumble through the apartment door.

They didn't take cover at the same time as they heard him enter. Until they heard him enter, they had no reason to take cover. First they heard him, and then, as a consequence of hearing him, they hid.

Sometimes, though, we do actually have two things happening at the same time. We need to understand when it's alright to use words like *as* in deep POV and when it's not.

Example time again.

As the basketball shot toward me, I threw my arms in front of my face.

Because the basketball flying through the air takes time, I can shield my face while the basketball is coming at me. The two do actually happen simultaneously.

Even if we do have two things that actually happen at the same time, my recommendation is to try to avoid connecting them with *as* because the reader's experience isn't "at the same time." Their experience is still linear. Because of the nature of reading, we can't experience two things at the same time. We experience them in the order they appear on the page. For this reason, we're best to put the action that ends quickest first and then connect them with a different conjunction.

I also recommend against the above *as* construction because it feels slower. So if we want to represent a quick action, like a flying basketball, we'd be better to write it this way.

The basketball shot toward me, and I threw my arms in front of my face.

This version still maintains cause and effect, action, and reaction. The basketball is flying toward me, and as a consequence of seeing it coming, I throw my arms in front of my face to protect myself.

However, in this situation, even though I personally prefer the second way for the reasons mentioned, it's up to your preference which one you want to use. Both are correct.

Cause-and-effect errors can be sneaky, though. If we've written a sentence where two things could be happening at the same time, that doesn't mean we're safe. We might still have reversed the natural order.

Once again, we'll look at an example so you can see what I mean.

My mouth went dry and a heavy weight settled in my chest as he led me down the hall to meet my birth mother for the first time.

Technically, this can be happening at the same time. There's time for something to happen as she's walking.

But here's the problem: Our sentence structure still needs to reflect the natural order. Even if we want to express that something is happening at the same time, when we write it, we need to give the reader the cause before we give them the effect.

In the above example, we find out our narrator's mouth is dry and she feels a heavy weight on her chest, but the reader will feel ungrounded because they have no idea what's causing it. Any time the reader loses connection to the viewpoint character and immersion in the story, it's a bad thing, and even more so when we're writing in deep POV.

You'll find this in your writing when your words express that one thing happened temporally before the other, but in the sentence you've reversed them. So you're saying A happened before B, but in your sentence what you've written is "B happened because of A."

You need to write down the cause (A) before the effect (B).

Before we move on, let's quickly go back to the example above and see one possible way we could rewrite it, keeping this in mind.

He led me down the hall to meet my birth mother. My mouth went dry and a heavy weight settled in my chest.

Same meaning, but now we're solidly in deep POV.

(If you need more help with grammar in your fiction, you might want to take a look at my co-written book *Grammar for Fiction Writers: A Busy Writer's Guide*.)

AVOID MADE/CAUSED-TYPE SENTENCES

This technique extends further than sentences including *made* or *caused*, but once you understand the principle behind these, you'll be able to apply it to all sentences that would fall into this category.

Made and *caused* are what's called causative verbs. You don't have to remember the term. You just need to understand what purpose they serve within the English language to understand why they violate deep POV.

Causative verbs are used to indicate that something helps to make something else happen. It describes cause and effect. Examples include *cause, allow, help, have, enable, keep, hold, let, force, require,* and *make.*

These are a problem because they often tell the reader that a result happened, rather than allowing the reader to experience the result at the same time as the character. In other words, it adds an additional layer of distance, which is the bane of deep POV.

Because everything is clearer with examples, it's time for some examples.

He tossed her the rope, allowing her to climb up.

It doesn't matter whether he's the viewpoint character or she is. This violates deep POV either way. We see him throw the rope, but we don't see her climb up. Instead we've been told what result the tossing of the rope will have.

Here's one possible way to fix this.

He tossed her the rope, and she climbed up.

I know this concept can be a tricky one because, as authors, we know what we meant. But deep POV isn't about us. It's about the viewpoint character. How about another example?

A loud noise above caused her to look up.

Like the previous example, this sentence tells us what happened because of the loud noise, but it doesn't show it to us in the way that the character would experience it.

I'll show you how we might fix this.

A loud noise rattled the ceiling above her. She glanced up.

We could have fixed that sentence in many different ways, so please don't get caught up in the way I did it. What I want you to notice is how we now actually see the viewpoint character look up.

In deep POV, we have to make sure we actually show things happening rather than merely telling the reader that an action was going to allow another or explaining the result.

DON'T EXPLAIN MOTIVATIONS USING "TO" PHRASES

Explaining motivations using a "to" phrase is the evil twin of made/caused-type sentences. "To" sentences tell us *why* a character did an action, but they don't show the action actually taking place. In deep POV, that's a problem.

Pay attention to the bolded and underlined part of this paragraph.

> She went to the closet **to grab her shotgun** and hunkered down behind the overturned table. The barricaded door wouldn't keep them out forever, and she planned to be ready.

Most of this is fine—except for the part underlined and bolded. The problem is that we don't actually see her grab the shotgun. We're told *why* she went to the closet, and then she's settling in to defend herself, but we missed the part where she actually got the gun. We've been removed one step from the character.

We're also telling instead of showing, and while we might be able to get away with this type of sentence once in a while in a farther narrative distance, it's a no-no in deep POV.

I'll give you another example.

Breaking Deep POV: She grabbed her bow **to shoot the deer**. The arrow arced through the air and lodged in the animal's throat. It sank to its knees. Dinner was served.

Once again, the problem is that we don't actually see her shoot. We're told *why* she grabbed her bow, and then the arrow is flying, but we've skipped the part when she fires the shot.

In Deep POV: She grabbed her bow, aimed for the deer's heart, and released the string. The arrow arced through the air and lodged in the animal's throat. It sank to its knees. Dinner was served.

AVOID WORDS THAT DENOTE TIME

By *words that denote time*, I don't mean time-of-the-day words. The words I'm referring to are ones like *suddenly, immediately, before,* and *after*.

I'll give an example for each one and explain why these are problematic in deep POV. (They're also showing rather than telling, so once you master this, you'll have improved two skills at once.)

We'll look at *before* and *after* first since the problem with them is the same.

The governor shook Angie's hand before giving her the medal.

This adds narrative distance because, instead of seeing it play out, we're given an order of events. It's not in the moment. When we're experiencing life, we don't think about something happening *before* or *after* something else.

The next problem word is *immediately*. Like so many other problem words, *immediately* tells the reader what's happening rather than allowing them to watch it play out in real time. We lose the real time aspect that we want in deep POV.

Beyond this, *immediately* isn't necessary. Take a look at the two examples below and think about whether there's any difference between them in terms of meaning (that is, in terms of what happens). Hint: There isn't.

> **Example A:** He set the gun down on the table, and I immediately grabbed it.

> **Example B:** He set the gun down on the table, and I grabbed it.

Because we don't show a pause or a hesitation, Example B shows the reader the exact same thing as Example A, without the intrusive *immediately*.

Suddenly works in a similar way to *immediately*. It's usually added to indicate the character was caught off guard, but it's telling you that the character was caught unawares by what happened rather than showing it.

We'll create a character named Candace for this example. Candace is hiding in an old boat shed from whatever pursuer you'd like to imagine. It could be zombies, a crazy stalker intent on making her his slave, or the mob who wants to knock her off because she witnessed something she shouldn't have.

In the boat shed, the only weapon she can find is a harpoon gun. She doesn't know how to work it.

Example A:

> Candace tugged on what appeared to be the trigger, but nothing happened. She pulled the trigger again. Still nothing.

So much for that idea. She dropped the rusted piece of junk back into the bottom of the row boat.

The harpoon gun fired suddenly. She stumbled backward and the harpoon lodged in the wall.

Example B:

Candace tugged on what appeared to be the trigger, but nothing happened. She pulled the trigger again. Still nothing.

So much for that idea. She dropped the rusted piece of junk back into the bottom of the row boat.

The harpoon gun fired. She stumbled backward and the harpoon lodged in the wall.

We know from the way it's written that the gun fired suddenly. We don't need to be told that it was sudden. Adding *suddenly* also adds a layer of distance and destroys the immediacy of the event. This is the irony of words like this. They're often meant to make the writing feel more immediate, and instead, they do the opposite.

CHAPTER NINE

Take It to the Page

IN EACH OF MY *BUSY WRITER'S GUIDES*, I LIKE to include checklists, questions, or other editing helps to make it easier for you to apply what you've learned to your own project. In many of my books, I include a Take It to the Page section at the end of every chapter.

In other cases, I leave the Take It to the Page section until the end. When I do this, it's because you need to understand the topic as a whole before you start making changes, or it's because it would be inefficient to have you do them at the end of each chapter due to overlap between the concepts. For deep POV, it's a little of both.

If you'd like a downloadable/printable copy of the Take It to the Page exercises, you can find them at www.marcykennedy.com/deepPOV.

*The password is **perspective**.*

PART A

We're going to start with some of the big-picture problems. The rationale behind this is that there's no use fixing the little issues until the big ones are taken care of.

In Part B, many of the editing steps will have shortcuts you can use to spot problem areas and save time. Unfortunately, the steps within Part A don't have similar editing hacks to make our lives easier. I will suggest ways to decide if each one is a problem area for you to pay more attention to or if you can move on, confident that this isn't an area you struggle with.

Step 1 – Are all your viewpoint characters necessary, or do you need to reduce the number of viewpoint characters?

We need to start with this step before any of the others because, if we're going to rewrite scenes to switch the viewpoint character, we need to do that before making any other changes within individual sentences.

In deep POV, we want to write our story with the fewest number of viewpoint characters possible. The rough guideline I gave is a maximum of three, but part of the purpose of these questions is to make sure that we've thought through our decisions and have good reasons for making the choices we make. Then, even if we decide to go against conventional advice, we can have more confidence that we're making the best choice for our story.

Start by writing down your viewpoint characters. If you have three or fewer and they're the main character, the antagonist, and the most important secondary character (often the love interest), then you can safely skip this step. If you have more than three or one of them is a minor character, keep going.

How many scenes/chapters have you given to each viewpoint character? There's no hard line here where "with only X scenes to their name, this character should be removed as a viewpoint character." So please, take this as a guideline that says you should look at these characters. It is **not** a rule that says you must remove them. If a character only has five or fewer scenes to their name, you need to look closely at them. Could those scenes be given to another character without losing anything important?

For each remaining viewpoint character, ask yourself these questions:

Does this character influence the plot? If the character doesn't influence the outcome of the plot, then they probably don't deserve to be a viewpoint character.

Does this character play a role at the climax of the novel? If they don't have a role in the "final battle," then they are questionable as a viewpoint character.

Does this character have a strong reason for being a viewpoint character? Each viewpoint character we include needs to have goals, motivations, and stakes within the story and to give a valuable perspective on the situation.

Step 2 – Do you have head-hopping or baton passes?

Read over two to three chapters in your story. Have you used a proper transition each time you've switched viewpoints? (If you don't know what I mean by proper transitions, please read Appendix D.)

If you haven't used proper transitions, rewrite the chapter to use proper transitions. If you find many times when you've switched without a proper transition, this is a clue that you probably struggle with head-hopping or baton passes and should do this check for the remainder of your book.

Step 3 – Have you withheld information from the reader that the viewpoint character would have known?

You should be able to figure this out by thinking about your story and the secrets you wanted to keep.

If you have wrongfully withheld information, then you need to rewrite the necessary sections so that you're not violating deep POV in order to deceive the reader. Another way to handle this would be to switch the viewpoint to a character who doesn't know the information you wish to withhold.

Step 4 – Look at the first sentence of each scene. Is the viewpoint character clear within the first sentence?

If not, rewrite the opening sentences to make the viewpoint character immediately clear.

Step 5 – How much direct internal dialogue have you used?

You probably already know if you lean towards writing direct internal dialogue or not. If not, skip this step.

If you do and you've formatted it with italics, it should be easy to see by skimming your work. Change as much of it as possible to indirect internal dialogue. (When writing in deep POV, you can often do this by simply changing the tense and person.)

If you haven't formatted it properly, this step will unfortunately take more time.

Step 6 – Have you resorted to forecasting to add tension?

Because of the various forms forecasting can take, there's no quick check for these. They usually appear at the beginning or end of a scene, so that's the best place to look if you're short on time. Have you added in a line or two to try to tease the reader about what's ahead?

If you find one, look at what came before it. Why did you feel the need to add the forecasting? That will help you see the weakness in the story that you need to fix so that you can also remove the forecasting.

PART B

Now we're moving on to the word-by-word changes that can enhance or destroy deep POV. Maybe of these come with what I call editing hacks—way to use the search feature on your word processing program to find most of the problem areas. These shortcuts won't catch absolutely every instance, but they'll come pretty close. This will make your final read-through a single-pass prospect where you can catch the remaining details. (More on this when we reach Part C.)

Step 1 – If you've already worked through the practical exercises in my books *Showing and Telling in Fiction* or *Point of View in Fiction*, then this step might look familiar. It also might seem long, but it's going to help you fix a lot of issues at once. You'll catch emotion-telling in your viewpoint character, and you'll catch point-of-view errors where you've shared the feelings of a non-viewpoint character. (We talked about these in Chapter 4 and Chapter 7.) One of the ways to be efficient with our time is to take care of two potential issues at once.

Run a search for the emotion-themed words in the following list. These are by no means the only words for emotions, but they'll help you catch the most common ones. You might also want to try variations on the word or try typing in the root of the word—for example, type in *sad*, not *sadness*, because a search for *sad* will show you *sad, sadness, sadly*, etc. as long as you *don't* select Whole Words Only.

If this emotion is attributed to your viewpoint character, are you naming the emotion the character is feeling? Figure out your character's root emotion, the nuances of it, and why they're feeling it, and then create a fresh way to show that emotion to the reader.

If this emotion is attributed to a non-viewpoint character, use one of the guiding principles explained in Chapter Four to fix the error.

You can create a macro in Microsoft Word to search for multiple words at once. If you don't know how to do this, check out this excellent post from Jami Gold called "Fix Showing vs. Telling with Macros & Word Lists." You could also do the words one at a time, but macros make it much faster.

afraid

agitated

alarmed

amazed

amused

angry

anguish

annoyed

anxious

ashamed

bitter

bored

calm

cautious

cheerful

comfortable

compassion

concerned

confident

confused

contempt

curious

defeated

defensive

depressed

desperate

determined

disappointed

disgusted

disillusioned

dismayed

disoriented

distrust

doubtful

dread

eager

embarrassed

enthusiastic

envious

excited

exhausted

frustrated

grateful

grief

grumpy

guilty

happy

hateful

helpless

hesitant

hopeful/hopeless

horrified

hostile

humiliated

hurt

impatient

indifferent

insecure

insulted

interested

irritated

jealous

joyful

lonely

mad

nervous

nostalgic

numb

optimistic

outraged

overwhelmed

panic

paranoid

pity

proud

rage

regretful

rejected

relaxed

relieved

reluctant

remorseful

resentful

resigned

restless

revulsion

sad

satisfied

scornful

self-conscious

shame

shocked

skeptical

smug

sorrowful

spiteful

stressed

stunned

surprised

suspicious

sympathetic

tired

uncomfortable

vengeful

wary

weary

worried

Step 2 – Search for the words in the following list. Have you used these words to tell the reader that a non-viewpoint character is thinking or noticing something? Have you used these words to tell the reader what your viewpoint character is thinking, rather than showing them think it? In that case, they should be removed/changed. Similarly to the previous step, we're taking care of two issues at once with this search.

believed

noticed

realized

wondered

thought

knew

remembered

recalled

reviewed

considered

Step 3 – Deep POV errors involving motivations belonging to non-viewpoint characters are one of the more difficult instances to catch because there's no easy way to use the search or find features of your word processing program. But we can start by using MS Word's Find feature to search for a few phrases that often go along with this type of error:

at the sight of/sound of

because

caught his/her eye

caught his/her attention

to (do something) – E.g., James scowled at Christine and reached over **to brush** dirt off her shirt sleeve. (Christine, the viewpoint character, can't know what he was intending when he reached. We're telling his motivation instead of showing his action.)

Step 4 – The words in this list are indicators that we've shown something the viewpoint character wasn't aware of. If you find them, rewrite the passage.

unknowingly

didn't notice

unconsciously

unaware

not realizing

Step 5 – Run a search for titles and relational names (e.g., sister, brother, teacher, doctor) that you might have used in your book. Check each of these to see if they represent a deep POV error.

Step 6 – Think about your book. Have you potentially called a character by different names throughout the book? Decide on what you'd like this character to be called (or what they'll be consistently called by each other character during that character's viewpoint scenes) and use the find feature in your word processing program to locate the variations that you need to change.

If you plan to use only one name for the character, you can use Find and Replace to speed up the process of making name usage consistent. (You might do this if you have only one viewpoint character or if all your viewpoint characters would refer to this person in the same way. Just be careful to select Whole Words Only so that "He stepped onto the mat" doesn't become "He stepped onto the Andrew.")

Step 7 – Do a search for the words *saw, smelled, tasted,* and *heard.* (If you're writing in present tense, you'll need to change the tense to match.)

Have you used these words as part of a simile or to try to describe one of the five senses? If they're part of a simile, move on to the next one. If you've used them to try to describe one of the five senses, can you make it more vivid and immediate by rewriting the sentence without *saw, smelled, tasted,* or *heard?*

Step 8 – Do a search for the word *felt.* (If you're writing in present tense, you'll need to change the tense to match.)

Have you used *felt* as part of a simile or to try to describe one of the five senses? If you've used it as part of a simile, move on to the next one. If you've used it to try to describe one of the five senses, can you make it more vivid and immediate by rewriting the sentence without *felt*?

Have you used this word to name an emotion? (E.g., "She felt sad over the death of her daughter.") This will help you catch any instances of naming emotions that you might have missed earlier. Figure out what your character is feeling (and why), and then create a fresh way to show that emotion to the reader.

Step 9 – Run a search for dialogue tags. This step might take more or less work depending on how you've been handling your dialogue tags.

If you've used creative dialogue tags, you have a bigger job ahead of you. If you know that you haven't used creative dialogue tags, skip down until the part where you see **Removing Regular Dialogue Tags**. For those of you who have used creative dialogue tags or aren't sure, keep reading.

When you have a character hiss, growl, beg, demand, or (insert another descriptor here) a sentence, you've used a creative dialogue tag. They violate the "show, don't tell" principle and, most of the time, they also violate deep POV. They're usually a sign of weak dialogue. (If you need more help with dialogue, take a look at my book *Dialogue: A Busy Writer's Guide*.)

So we need to cut creative dialogue tags first. Search for these words and cut them. You will often have to rewrite the dialogue to keep the meaning clear. If you absolutely feel you still need a tag, use *said*, *asked*, or one denoting volume (e.g., *shouted*, *whispered*). We'll look at cutting those out next.

acknowledged

admitted

agreed

angled

answered

argued

babbled

barked

begged

bellowed

bemoaned

blurted

blustered

bragged

breathed

commented

complained

confessed

cried

croaked

crooned

crowed

demanded

denied

drawled

echoed

faltered

fumed

giggled

groaned

growled

grumbled

heckled

hinted

hissed

howled

implored

inquired

inserted

interjected

interrupted

jested

laughed

mumbled

murmured

muttered

nagged

offered

opined

orated

pleaded

pouted

promised

queried

questioned

quipped

quoted

raged

ranted

reiterated

remembered

replied

requested

retorted

roared

ruminated

sang

scolded

screamed

screeched

shouted

shrieked

sighed

snarled

snickered

snorted

sobbed

sputtered

stammered

stuttered

threatened

thundered

told

wailed

warned

whimpered

whined

wondered

yelped

Removing Regular Dialogue Tags

Now that we've gotten rid of the creative dialogue tags, run a search for the following words.

said

asked

whispered

yelled

shouted

Do you absolutely need each tag you've used, or can you remove them without confusing the reader?

Step 10 – Have you overused the viewpoint character's name in their scenes? (If you're writing in first person, skip this step. It only applies to people writing in third person who can call their character by their name or by a personal pronoun.)

You can make this easier by using the Find and Replace feature in MS Word to highlight your viewpoint character's name. Click on Replace. Add the character's name to the "Find what:" field and the "Replace with:" field. Make sure your cursor is still in "Replace with:" and then click "More>>". Under Format, choose Highlight. Then tell it to Replace All.

This method will highlight every time your character's name appears. It helps you quickly and easily see if you've overused your viewpoint character's name, and you can replace it with the proper pronoun in spots where it wouldn't cause confusion.

Step 11 – Describing a change in a character's skin tone can be fine or it can violate deep POV, depending on whether or not we're describing the viewpoint character.

Search for the following words with Whole Words Only deselected so you're shown all variants:

pale

red

blue

green

white

pink

Step 12 – The lips and eyes are areas where we can accidentally slip into describing how our viewpoint character looked rather than having them act.

Searching for the words in this list will show you all the times these show up. Only the ones describing the viewpoint character might be a problem. Remember to look at the context. Are they acting or are they being described as if someone else were looking at them?

lips

eye

smile

smirk

frown

muscle

pulse

The last two points will help you catch those times when you might have a muscle twitching in a cheek or a pulse beating in your viewpoint character's neck or at their temple.

Step 13 – Run a search for *the night before, the day before,* or *the next day.* If you find any, replace them with *last night, yesterday, tomorrow,* or another character-centric option.

Step 14 – In this step, you're going to try to find places where you've created an error by violating the temporal order.

Here's what you should enter.

Find: as

Replace: AS

(Make sure you put a space in front of and behind *as* or that you select Whole Words Only, otherwise your search will show you every time an *a* appears next to an *s*.)

By replacing the smaller case *as* with all caps, they'll jump out at you. Alternatively, you could highlight them the way we did with character names earlier.

For every AS, ask yourself the following questions.

Have you reversed cause and effect? If so, make sure you have the action come first, followed by the reaction.

Have you created a situation where two things are grammatically happening at the same time that can't actually happen at the same time? Rewrite it as two separate sentences to show the real sequence of events.

For any *as* that serves a legitimate purpose in the sentence, simply change it back to the lowercase.

Repeat this process for *when* and *while*.

Step 15 – Run a search for variations on *cause, allow, help, enable, keep, hold, let, force, require,* and *make*.

You might have to alter the search parameters a little depending on the tense of your story and how you might have used these words. For example, if you think you're prone to using *make* variations, you'll want to search for both *making* and *made*. Another way to speed this up is to make sure Whole Words Only isn't selected. By doing so, when you search for *allow*, you'll see instances of *allow, allowing,* and *allowed*.

Rewrite the instances you find to show the action rather than telling the result.

Step 16 – Search for *suddenly, immediately, before,* and *after*. Can you remove them from the sentence or change the sentence so they're unnecessary?

Step 17 – Choose three to four chapters randomly from your book. You're going to read them through and highlight the following elements:

Visceral reactions

Motivations

Character thoughts

Descriptions

The colors you choose to use don't matter as long as each is highlighted in a different color. The idea here is to allow you to see patterns and to quickly check for potential problems. If you don't see problems on these pages, then you can be fairly secure in believing that your other chapters don't have major problems as well. If you do find problems, then you'll want to take the time to review that element in the rest of your book.

For Visceral Reactions: You should now be able to see if you either have none, have too many, or have a tendency to place them in inappropriate spots.

For Motivations: You should be able to see if you've been including them. By reading what you've highlighted, you should also be able to tell if you've written them in a character-authentic way or if they sound like author telling.

For Character Thoughts: Do you have too many paragraphs in a row without any externals? Or do you go for paragraphs without your viewpoint character thinking at all? Are the thoughts happening when your viewpoint character would naturally think them, in the way they would be thinking them?

For Descriptions: Are the descriptions in these chapters colored by the opinions and emotions of the viewpoint character?

PART C

I call this the final step because it's something you'll do when you're reading through your book for a complete pass. (You do plan to read through your book in a couple of sittings the way a reader would, don't you? If not, you should. It's one step we should never skimp on, no matter how tight our time is.)

These are items where there's no quick check and no shortcut. You'll only see them as you read.

I recommend that you flag anything you find by using the Comment feature in MS Word (or something similar if you're using a different program) rather than stopping to fix each item as you find it. A full read needs to be done in a short span of time to replicate the reader experience. If you're stopping to make corrections, you won't be able to do that.

As you read, watch for the following:

- Areas where you have the viewpoint character think about something they're familiar with – did you give them a solid reason to be thinking about it?
- Areas where you've magically filled a gap in the viewpoint character's knowledge so they're naming or understanding something they have no previous experience with.
- Spots where you've used the article *the* even though the viewpoint character was experiencing something new.
- Body parts that seem to be acting of their own volition.
- Similes or metaphors that don't fit the character thinking them.
- That your viewpoint character feels like they're at the center (remember *here* vs. *there*).
- How you've used evidential adverbs and modal verbs (such as *seemed* or *appeared*). Did you use them to make

it clear when your viewpoint character is guessing or making an assumption? Have you only used them when a situation could be interpreted in various ways rather than when it's a fact? Take a peek back at Chapter Six if you forget how these work.

Now that you understand deep POV, spots that slipped by you in your earlier checks will also probably jump out at you as well.

Direct and Indirect Internal Dialogue

T HIS APPENDIX IS AN EXCERPT FROM MY
book *Internal Dialogue.* I wanted to include it as an extra here
because I know not everyone will have read that book before
reading this one.

Writing in deep POV requires you to use internal dialogue and
to use it properly. While I can't re-cover everything about internal
dialogue in this book (that'd be repetitive, wouldn't it?), I did want to
briefly look at one aspect that tends to confuse writers the most—
direct vs. indirect internal dialogue.

A common misconception about deep POV is that you need to
use direct internal dialogue. The opposite is actually true. When
writing in deep POV, we should stick to indirect internal dialogue as
much as possible.

Why? Well, in deep POV, everything we hear is filtered through our viewpoint character. Much of what ends up on the page is, in fact, internal dialogue. If we made all of it direct internal dialogue, it'd be awkward and jarring. Their internal dialogue will blend in with what's happening in a very natural way if we're writing in indirect internal dialogue.

So this excerpt explains the difference between direct and indirect internal dialogue and how to write great indirect internal dialogue...

Indirect internal dialogue gives the reader an idea of the point-of-view character's thoughts, but not the exact words they're thinking.

Direct internal dialogue gives the reader the exact words that the point-of-view character is thinking. It's written in first person and present tense, regardless of the person and tense of the rest of the story.

Direct vs. indirect internal dialogue isn't a case of good vs. evil. Many authors use both within the same story, and when you're writing in deep POV, the line between the two is often fuzzy.

Under the umbrella of indirect internal dialogue, however, you do find good and bad. Indirect internal dialogue can easily turn into telling (rather than showing). If you don't know what I mean by showing and telling, please read Appendix B before continuing. You can also pick up a copy of my book *Showing and Telling in Fiction* for in-depth coverage.

To clarify what I mean, I'm going to walk you through some examples of bad indirect internal dialogue, good indirect internal dialogue, and direct internal dialogue.

For our first example, let's say we have a woman whose husband comes home, supposedly straight from work, but he smells strange, like lilies. You want to have her think about that and wonder why he smells like lilies, where he could have been to smell like lilies.

Keep in mind as I show you how this could be written that I'm showing you only a few possible ways to express this idea. How you personally might choose to express this idea as direct or indirect dialogue might not be the same as how I've chosen to do it. What I want you to pay attention to are the differences between the types of internal dialogue. That's the important part, and I'll point them out.

BAD Indirect Internal Dialogue:

> She wondered where he'd been that he came home smelling like lilies. She couldn't think of anywhere that smelled like that except a funeral parlor filled with flower arrangements.

In this example, we, the writers, have stepped between the character and the reader, and we're acting like a filter. Instead of allowing the reader access to the inside of the character and showing the reader what's going on behind the curtain (allowing the character to act as the filter), we're telling them what's going on.

A couple of things signal that this could be bad indirect internal dialogue. The first is the word *wondered*. Both the words *wondered* and *realized* can be an indicator that you're telling the reader the point-of-view character is realizing or wondering rather than showing them realize or showing them wonder.

Another red flag is the phrase *she couldn't think of*. A phrase like this doesn't always indicate bad indirect internal dialogue, but it means we should take a closer look. It suggests that we're telling the reader what our character couldn't do rather than showing our character trying and failing to do it.

Bad indirect internal dialogue has a distancing effect. It strips away the character's personality, making it lifeless. It's also unnecessary to write it this way. If we don't want to use direct internal dialogue, we have another option—turn it into good indirect internal dialogue.

Turning this into good indirect internal dialogue can be simple. All we need to do is rephrase it to remove the word *wondered* and make the event immediate rather than secondhand.

GOOD Indirect Internal Dialogue:

The stench of lilies clung to his clothes and hair. It seemed like a smell she should recognize, one she knew. The idea bounced around in her mind the same as a word that wouldn't come off the tip of her tongue when she needed it. It was too natural to be perfume. It didn't smell like any place they regularly went.

She shuddered. *Death.* He smelled like death, like a funeral parlor crowded with flower arrangements and a corpse.

A bit of direct internal dialogue sneaked into this paragraph with the word *death* (which I italicized). As I mentioned in the opening to this chapter, you'll often need to interweave direct and indirect internal dialogue for the best results.

What I want you to pay attention to here, though, is how removing the crutch of *wondered* pushes us to bring this internal dialogue to life for the reader. When we can't fall back on *wondered*, we have to think about the contents of what she was wondering and show her going through the process.

Those details are what differentiate good indirect internal dialogue from bad indirect internal dialogue. When we tell the reader that the character wondered something, it leaves too much room for misinterpretation and confusion. What if the reader doesn't guess correctly about what the character was wondering?

When you're trying to decide whether you've written good or bad indirect internal dialogue, ask yourself if it's clear what your character is thinking. The key to avoiding bad indirect internal dialogue is to ensure that we're giving enough details that the reader knows what's going on.

Before I show you an example of direct internal dialogue, I want to show you another version of good indirect internal dialogue. The previous example was from a more distant, limited third-person point of view. (In other words, we were hearing the story told from the perspective of a single character, but we weren't as tightly connected to her as we could have been.) The following example is indirect internal dialogue from a close third-person point of view, which is also known as writing in deep POV.

GOOD Indirect Internal Dialogue:

The suffocating stench of lilies clung to his clothes and hair, out of place among his usual coming-home-from-work scents of antiseptic soap and coffee.

She slowly pulled away from his hug. Shivers traced over her arms. She knew that smell. Not perfume. It was too natural for that, but it also wasn't an everyday odor. She wouldn't expect to run into it at the grocery store. Or the bank, either. It was rare. Heavy, warm, and sad.

Her breath tripped in her throat, and she stepped back. He smelled like death, like a corpse smothered in flower arrangements at a funeral parlor. The last time she'd smelled it was standing next to her mother's coffin, saying goodbye.

In this example, we hear her essentially saying to herself *I should recognize that smell*, and working through where she remembers it from in her own words.

Look at the specific word choices she makes—*suffocating, clung, death*. She associates the fragrance of lilies with grief and death. Those are her words. That's what would have gone through her head.

However, it's not direct internal dialogue because it's still written in past tense and third person. I wanted to show you this example before giving you an example of direct internal dialogue because it's important to see how blurry the line between direct and indirect internal dialogue can be when you're writing from a deep point of view.

Direct Internal Dialogue:

The suffocating stench of lilies clung to his clothes and hair, out of place among his usual coming-home-from-work scents of antiseptic soap and coffee.

She slowly pulled away from his hug. Shivers traced over her arms. *I know that smell. I should know that smell.*

Not perfume. It was too natural for that, but it also wasn't an everyday odor. She wouldn't expect to run into it at the grocery store. Or the bank, either. It was rare. Heavy, warm, and sad.

Her breath tripped in her throat, and she stepped back. *He smells like death, like a corpse smothered in flowers at a funeral parlor.* The last time she'd smelled that scent was standing next to her mother's coffin, saying goodbye.

You'll notice again that this weaves indirect and direct internal dialogue together. The direct internal dialogue is in present tense, is in first person, and is italicized.

The key to distinguishing between direct and indirect internal dialogue is that simple.

Is it in first person, present tense?

Yes – Then it's direct internal dialogue.

No – Then it's indirect internal dialogue.

Because this is an important concept, I'm going to give you another set of examples, starting off with bad indirect internal dialogue again.

BAD Indirect Internal Dialogue:

> Janie watched Frank hunched over the map and realized she'd never convince him to take the mountain path without a dang good reason. She needed him to take that mountain path or all the plans she'd made with Jake would be worth nothing. She had to convince Frank that the shelter provided by the caves outweighed the numerous disadvantages.

In this case, it's clear what the character is thinking. Janie knows Frank isn't going to go the way she wants him to and that will ruin all her plans.

What makes this bad indirect internal dialogue again is how far we're being held from the point-of-view character (Janie). We've told the reader she realized something rather than showing her realizing it. In other words, we're summarizing for the reader when we should be showing it happen in real time.

Then we're stating the goal and stakes. It's good to use internal dialogue to reveal our characters' goals and motivations, but we need to do it in the right way—a way that brings it to life for the reader. Those goals, motivations, and stakes should come across naturally as the character thinks about their situation rather than in a way that feels like the author is intruding to make sure the reader "gets it."

GOOD Indirect Internal Dialogue:

Frank hunched over the map, using his fingers to trace out the different options for their escape route. His hand never even veered in the direction of the mountain path. The mountains provided too many places for ambush, not to mention the bears and fewer chances at restocking along the way.

Janie gnawed on her bottom lip. Frank was practical. She could take advantage of that by giving him a good enough reason to take the mountain path anyway.

She laid her hand on top of the massive pile of gear. "If we carry all this, it's going to slow us down. We could leave at least half of it behind if we used the Danbury Ridge caves instead. And we'd be able to have a fire without lightin' ourselves up like a lighthouse beacon."

Let's look at this again, going into a deeper POV but still using indirect internal dialogue.

GOOD Indirect Internal Dialogue:

Frank hunched over the map, using his fingers to trace out the different options for their escape route. His hand never even veered in the direction of the mountain path.

Too many places for ambush in the mountains. Too many bears. No chance to restock. He didn't need to list the reasons out loud for her to know them. In any other situation, she would have agreed with him.

But Jake gave her one job—make sure Frank takes the mountain path.

She could do this. What one overwhelming advantage was there to taking that path over sticking to the plains? She bit her bottom lip. The caves.

She laid her hand on top of the massive pile of gear. "If we carry all this, it's going to slow us down. We could leave at least half of it behind if we used the Danbury Ridge caves instead. And we'd be able to have a fire without lightin' ourselves up like a lighthouse beacon."

Now I'll show you the same example rewritten as direct internal dialogue. The direct internal dialogue is italicized.

Direct Internal Dialogue:

Frank hunched over the map, using his fingers to trace out the different options for their escape route. His hand never even veered in the direction of the mountain path.

Too many places for ambush in the mountains. Too many bears. No chance to restock. He didn't need to list the reasons out loud for her to know them. In any other situation, she would have agreed with him.

But Jake gave her one job—make sure Frank takes the mountain path.

She scrubbed a hand under the brim of her hat. *I can do this. What one overwhelming advantage is there to taking that path over sticking to the plains?* She bit her bottom lip. *The caves.*

She laid her hand on top of the massive pile of gear. "If we carry all this, it's going to slow us down. We could leave at least half of it behind if we used the Danbury Ridge caves instead. And we'd be able to have a fire without lightin' ourselves up like a lighthouse beacon."

Let me give you one more example because I want you to see how the difference between indirect and direct internal dialogue can sometimes be minor.

Remember not to get caught up in the exact phrases I use. Instead, pay attention to the big-picture differences in the passages. This time I'm only going to show you good indirect internal dialogue compared to direct internal dialogue. I'll underline the internal dialogue in both examples.

Indirect Internal Dialogue:

A flush crept up the waitress' neck, and she blinked rapidly. Emily mouthed the words *I'm sorry*, but couldn't be sure if she noticed. The girl spun on her heel and scurried away.

Emily glared at Jared. "That was cruel."

"Lighten up." A smirk twisted his lips in a way she used to find endearing. "I was just teasing her."

Emily pushed her food away and closed her eyes. <u>Jerk. She never should have married him. But she'd taken vows and now she had no way out...and he knew it as well as she did.</u>

Direct Internal Dialogue:

A flush crept up the waitress' neck, and she blinked rapidly. Emily mouthed the words *I'm sorry*, but couldn't be sure if she noticed. The girl spun on her heel and scurried away.

She glared at Jared. "That was cruel."

"Lighten up." A smirk twisted his lips in a way she used to find endearing. "I was just teasing her."

Emily pushed her food away and closed her eyes. <u>*Jerk. I never should have married you. But I took vows and now I have no way out...and you know it as well as I do.*</u>

The difference between the two types of internal dialogue in this example is only in the person and tense.

Both indirect and direct internal dialogue are fine to use. The amount of each you include depends on your personal writing voice and the story you're writing.

The important thing to take away from this chapter is this—make sure that you're writing internal dialogue that gives a clear picture of the point-of-view character's thoughts. Vague internal dialogue doesn't move the story forward and can leave the reader confused.

Showing and Telling

THE FOLLOWING EXCERPTS COME FROM my book *Showing and Telling in Fiction*. Because I know that not everyone who reads this book will have also read that one, I decided it would help to include a bit about the topic here. Deep POV and showing rather than telling are intimately connected, so the better you understand one, the better you'll execute the other.

WHAT DO WE MEAN BY SHOWING?

Showing happens when we let the reader experience things for themselves, through the perspective of the characters. Jeff Gerke, former owner of Marcher Lord Press, explains showing in one simple question: **Can the camera see it?**[1]

While I love that way of looking at it, we'd really have to ask **can the camera see it, hear it, smell it, touch it, taste it, or think it?**

---

[1] Jeff Gerke, *The First 50 Pages* (Cincinnati: Writer's Digest Books, 2011), 40.

(And that would be a strange camera.) Because of that, I prefer to think about showing as being in a *Star Trek* holodeck.

For those of you who aren't as nerdy as I am, a holodeck is a virtual reality room where users can act as a character in a story, which is fully projected using photons and force fields. You can play Jane Eyre or *Twilight's* Bella or Lee Child's Jack Reacher.

What the user experiences is what they can see, hear, touch, taste, or smell. In holodecks, you can smell things and you can eat or drink "replicated" food. It's a completely immersive experience. To the holodeck user, the experience seems real in all respects. And if you turn the holodeck safety systems off, you can be injured or even die.

When you're faced with deciding whether something is showing or telling, ask yourself this question: **If this were a holodeck program, would I be able to experience this?**

Let's take a couple examples and test them out. A straightforward one first.

Kate realized she'd locked her keys in the car.

Now, you're standing in the holodeck. What do you experience? ...Nothing. We can't see "realized." We don't know how she knows her keys are locked in the car. Anything we might visualize is something we've had to add because the author didn't. There's no picture here.

Here's one possible showing version...

Kate yanked on the car door handle. The door didn't budge, and her keys dangled from the ignition. "Dang it!"

You don't have to tell us Kate realized her keys were locked inside her car because we're right there with her. We see her figure it out.

Let's take a more challenging example. This time you're in the holodeck, playing the character of Linda. (Remember that, since you're Linda, you can hear her thoughts, as well as see, smell, hear, taste, and feel what she does.)

First the "telling" version.

> Linda stood at the edge of the Grand Canyon. Though her head spun from the height, she was amazed by the grandeur of it and felt a sense of excitement. Finally she'd taken a big step toward overcoming her fear of heights.

What do you physically experience in the holodeck? Only the Grand Canyon. If you don't know what the Grand Canyon looks like, you can't see even that. None of the rest can appear around you. None of it is her thoughts. They're all abstractions. What does being amazed by the grandeur look like? What does excitement feel like? What does her fear of heights feel like?

If we're in the holodeck, it's going to play out something more like this...

> Linda gripped the damp metal railing that ringed the horseshoe-shaped walkway over the Grand Canyon. Her vision blurred, and she drew in a deep breath and puffed it out the way the instructor taught her in Lamaze class. If it worked for childbirth, it should work to keep her from passing out now. She forced her gaze down to the glass floor. Thick bands of rust red and tan alternated their way down canyon walls that looked as if they'd been chiseled by a giant sculptor. The shaking in her legs faded. She had to get a picture to take back to her kids.

You can see what's around Linda, and you sense her amazement at the size of the canyon, as well as feel her fear. Emotionally you move with her from fear to wonder to excitement as she thinks about sharing it with her children. We hear it in her thoughts. This is the trick to good internal dialogue. It's what your character is thinking at that moment, the way they would think it. It's like you've planted a listening device in their brain and can play their thoughts on a speaker.

So the next time you're not sure whether you're showing or telling, ask "What would I experience in a holodeck?" That's how you should write it if you want to show rather than tell.

WHAT IS TELLING?

The simple answer would be to say that telling is everything that's not showing, but that's not exact enough for me. What I like to do is compare telling and showing when defining telling.

If showing presents evidence to the reader and allows them to draw their own conclusions, telling dictates a conclusion to the reader, telling them what to believe. It states a fact.

Bob was angry...dictates a conclusion.

But what was the evidence?

Bob punched his fist into the wall.

The Black Plague ravaged the country...dictates a conclusion.

But what was the evidence?

You could describe men loading dead bodies covered in oozing black sores onto a wagon. Your protagonist could press a handkerchief filled with posies to her nose and mouth as she passes someone who's drawing in ragged, labored breaths.

Either of those details, or many others, would show the Black Death ravaging the country.

As-You-Know-Bob Syndrome

I N THE CHAPTER ON LIMITED KNOWLEDGE, I pointed out that a character won't think about something they're familiar with unless we give them a reason to do so.

A related writing craft issue is As-You-Know-Bob Syndrome. It's the dialogue version of what we were looking at for deep POV. The more we understand how this potential problem can come up in different areas and how to fix it when it does, the less likely we'll be to fall into the trap of sharing something our character wouldn't normally share.

What follows is an excerpt from *Dialogue: A Busy Writer's Guide*...

As the name suggests, As-You-Know-Bob Syndrome is when one character tells another character something they already know. It's done purely for the reader's benefit, and it's unnatural.

A character won't say something the character they're talking to already knows.

For example, a husband won't say to his wife, "When we bought this house two years ago, we emptied our savings for a down payment. We don't have anything left."

The wife already knows when the house was purchased. She knows they emptied their savings. She also knows they haven't been able to replace those savings yet.

Thus, her husband has no reason to say any of that.

Info dumps won't always be this obvious, but if you could add "as you know" to the front of whatever's being said, it's time to rewrite.

If it's common knowledge, it won't come up in conversation.

Let's say you have two sisters meeting to go out for lunch. One shows up at the other's door.

"Come on in, Susie. I'm just cleaning up the muddy paw prints left by our pit bull, Jasper."

It's common knowledge her sister owns a pit bull named Jasper. Her sister wouldn't feel the need to state it. She'd be more likely to say...

"Come in for a sec. I just have to clean up the mud the stupid dog tracked in again."

Even essential information needs to be given in a natural way. So if knowing that their dog is a pit bull named Jasper is essential to the story, you could write...

> A flash of fur tore across Ellen's freshly washed floor and threw itself at Susie.
> Susie shoved the dog down. "Off, Jasper."
> He dropped onto his back for a belly rub, tongue lolling out of his mouth.
> Ellen sighed. "Sorry about that. Did he get you dirty?"
> Susie shook her head and scratched Jasper behind the ear. Even if he had, a little mud never hurt anyone. "Any more trouble with the anti-pit bull crowd at the park? Brent said someone threatened to call the cops last week."

A character won't say something that isn't relevant to the conversation.

> "A hundred years ago, when the dam was constructed, this town was built on the dried-out flood plain. If the dam breaks, it'll wipe out the whole place."

Did you catch the sneaky insertion of backstory in adding "a hundred years ago"? What normal person would actually say that? Who would care how long ago the dam was built when the real issue is whether or not the town is about to be destroyed?

If we have two town residents talking, they also know the town is built on a flood plain. While that's relevant to the conversation, it violates the common knowledge rule. Find a more creative way to bring in the information.

HOW CAN WE AVOID AS-YOU-KNOW-BOB SYNDROME?

Figure out what information is essential to the scene and only include that.

Let's look at an example where two brothers are being held captive. Their kidnapper leaves them locked in a room during the day while he goes to work.

> "Remember the trick you used on Aunt Angie that summer we stayed with her? You rigged the doorknob so it wouldn't close securely when she tried to lock us in our room at night. We could do something like that."

This is an info dump because both characters already know the specifics. They'd be more likely to say...

> "What if you did what you used to do to Aunt Angie?"

The problem is that's not enough info for the reader.

So we pull out what's essential. When they were with Aunt Angie doesn't matter. Why she locked them up doesn't matter. What's really essential for the reader to know is that one brother knows how to rig a door so that even when it looks locked, it can actually be forced open.

> "What if you did what you used to do to Aunt Angie?"
> Frank crinkled his forehead. "He never leaves us alone long enough. It took me a whole day to file the ridges off the doorknob latch."

But sometimes you really do need a character to talk about something they wouldn't normally talk about or to say something the listener already knows. What then?

Pick a fight.

Fighting characters will dredge up things the other character already knows and use them as weapons against each other.

Let's go back to our earlier example of the husband and wife (Nathan and Linda) who bought the house two years ago, drained their savings, and haven't been able to replace their savings yet. Say we have a scene happening where the husband finally quit the high-paying job where he's treated like a doormat, but he did it without talking to his wife first. She's angry because they won't be able to make their mortgage payments on her salary alone.

> Nathan balled up the resignation letter. "You're the one who wanted this house in the first place. I was happy in our apartment."
>
> "We bumped into each other just trying to dress in the morning. We couldn't raise a family there."
>
> "We could have waited at least. We shouldn't have rushed into a house and drained our savings. I wanted to stay in the job I loved."
>
> "So it's all my fault?" Linda grabbed a club from his golf bag by the door. "We'd have plenty saved if you'd give up a golf game now and then."

Same information, much more exciting way of sharing it. (We also learn more about the characters and their relationship.)

Introduce a character to "play dumb."

A "dumb" character is one who's new to the situation and doesn't know what the others do. They don't actually have to be unintelligent. They can be highly intelligent in other areas. They just need to be out of their element or uneducated in this particular scenario. (Jeff Gerke, former editor-in-chief of Enclave Publishing, calls this a dump puppet.)

In the movie *Twister*, Dr. Melissa Reeves functions in this role because she doesn't know anything about tornadoes. She asks questions no other character would ask because they already know all about tornadoes. Through her, we learn the information we need to learn.

This was also part of the brilliance in how J.K. Rowling wrote her *Harry Potter* stories. Even though Harry was born from magical parents, he knew nothing of the magical world prior to coming to Hogwarts because he was raised by Muggles (non-magical folk). In other words, Harry learned about the world at the same time we did, and gave Rowling a natural, believable way to tell us what we needed to know.

Often you can also use a child in this role because children are naturally curious and haven't yet developed the social filter that holds many adults back. My best friend's seven-year-old daughter once said to another woman, "I love your skirt. It looks just like a towel." Children can get away with things that adults can't.

Proper and Improper Transitions

HAVING MORE THAN ONE VIEWPOINT character and switching between viewpoint characters is a normal part of writing fiction. Some stories need more than one viewpoint character to reach their full potential. What we need to do is make sure we switch between viewpoint characters correctly.

This appendix is an excerpt from my book *Point of View in Fiction.*

IMPROPER TRANSITIONS

Switching viewpoints within a paragraph is head-hopping, but switching viewpoints between paragraphs is also an improper transition. If we're writing in first person or third person, we can't use one viewpoint character in our first paragraph and then switch to another viewpoint character in the next paragraph. That's still head-hopping.

As a way around this, some authors use what's called a baton pass.

A baton pass happens when we use an object in the environment to signal a viewpoint shift between two characters. I've bolded the baton pass in the following passage.

> Emily dropped two sugar cubes into the bottom of the mug and poured in the steaming tea. Heaven forbid her mother be asked to add the sugar cubes after the tea was in the cup like a normal person would. Thank God she only had to deal with her mother's quirks on holidays anymore. **She pushed the cup across the table to her mother.**
>
> **Alice accepted the cup and swirled the tea around inside.** If the look on Emily's face at having to prepare the tea the proper way was any indication, her next request was going to go over about as well as if she asked the ungrateful girl to slit her own wrists. "I've been to see the doctor again, and the news isn't good."

In this passage, we switch viewpoint characters from Emily to her mother Alice, using the mug of tea as our baton.

I have this listed as an improper transition because most people, myself included, consider a baton pass to be an insufficient transition to justify a change in the viewpoint character.

PROPER TRANSITIONS

For proper transitions, I'm going to move from the most clear and obvious to a more subtle method.

So the first way to properly transition between viewpoint characters is simply to switch during a chapter break. This is the easiest for the reader to handle because they have to slightly reorient themselves between chapters anyway. It doesn't seem jarring to be in a new point of view when a new chapter starts.

A very similar situation is when we have a scene break within a chapter. Scene breaks are often marked with asterisks or some other symbol. When we do this, we need to be careful that our scenes are long enough and that we don't switch viewpoint characters every scene. We want our reader to have a chance to settle in.

Sometimes, though, we need to switch our viewpoint within a scene. We can do this as long as we insert a blank line. That's an indicator to the reader to expect a switch. Do this very sparingly, as it can feel like the scene has stopped dead in order for us to swap viewpoint characters. (Some authors will use asterisks or some other symbol to signify these switches as well, since they're easier to spot than a blank line. That's fine too, and it's actually my personal preference. When in doubt, I like to err on the side of clarity.)

The final way to transition is to use a camera zoom out. This is tricky for new writers to master, so my advice is that, if you want to do this, pay attention to how it's handled in published works.

What basically happens here is that, for a minute, we're going to be disembodied. The reader is going to leave the current viewpoint character's head, float without attachment for a sentence or two, and then reconnect to another viewpoint character. We usually only want to do this when we're changing the location as well.

Let me show you how it looks.

Elaine twirled the dial on the safe and the door popped. Finally. Three months of work, but it was all going to be worth it once she got her hands on those files. She swung the door open. The safe was empty.

Across town, her former partner leaned over the phone records and photos that proved the sen-

ator's infidelities. Grant waited for his digital camera to focus and snapped close-up images of the first paper. He couldn't keep a smile from his lips. What he wouldn't give to see Elaine's face when she found the safe empty. Served her right for cutting him out of this job.

That single bolded sentence is a camera zoom out. For that single sentence, we're on the move and not connected to a character just for the duration of the transition. As soon as we hit Grant, we're right back in his head and his viewpoint.

Camera zoom outs need to be used strategically. We need to ask ourselves whether we really need them or if we could simply drop in a scene or chapter break and end up with the same result.

If we're writing in deep POV, we're best off avoiding camera zoom outs because they leave us without a narrator, which feels odd in deep POV and acts as a flashing light reminding the reader that they're reading a story.

Other Books by Marcy Kennedy

FOR WRITERS

Internal Dialogue

Internal dialogue is the voice inside our heads that we can't ignore, even when we want to. We second-guess ourselves, pass judgment on the world around us, and are at our most emotionally vulnerable. And the same needs to be true for our characters.

Internal dialogue is one of the most powerful tools in a fiction writer's arsenal. It's an advantage we have over TV and movie script writers and playwrights. It's also one of the least understood and most often mismanaged elements of the writing craft.

In *Internal Dialogue: A Busy Writer's Guide*, you'll learn...

- the difference between internal dialogue and narration,
- best practices for formatting internal dialogue,
- ways to use internal dialogue to advance your story,
- how to balance internal dialogue with external action,

- clues to help you decide whether you're overusing or underusing internal dialogue,
- tips for dealing with questions in your internal dialogue,
- and much more!

Showing and Telling in Fiction

You've heard the advice "show, don't tell" until you can't stand to hear it anymore. Yet fiction writers of all levels still seem to struggle with it.

There are three reasons for this. The first is that this isn't an absolute rule. Telling isn't always wrong. The second is that we lack a clear way of understanding the difference between showing and telling. The third is that we're told "show, don't tell," but we're often left without practical ways to know how and when to do that, and how and when not to. So that's what this book is about.

Chapter One defines showing and telling and explains why showing is normally better.

Chapter Two gives you eight practical ways to find telling that needs to be changed to showing and guides you in understanding how to make those changes.

Chapter Three explains how telling can function as a useful first-draft tool.

Chapter Four goes in-depth on the seven situations when telling might be a better choice than showing.

Chapter Five provides you with practical editing tips to help you take what you've learned to the pages of your current novel or short story.

Showing and Telling in Fiction: A Busy Writer's Guide also includes three appendices covering how to use *The Emotion Thesaurus*, dissecting an example so you can see the concepts of showing vs. telling in action, and explaining the closely related topic of As-You-Know-Bob Syndrome.

Dialogue

To write great fiction, you need to know how to write dialogue that shines.

You know the benefits strong dialogue can bring to a story—a faster pace, greater believability, increased tension, and even humor.

But you might not know how to achieve it.

In *Dialogue: A Busy Writer's Guide*, writing instructor and fiction editor Marcy Kennedy brings her years of experience into showing you how to write dialogue that grabs readers and keeps them turning pages.

Inside you'll discover…

- how to format your dialogue to keep it clear and easy to follow,
- tricks to avoid the dreaded As-You-Know-Bob Syndrome,
- how to use dialogue to manage your pace, increase tension, and bring your characters to life,
- the secrets to dealing with dialogue challenges such as dialect, starting a chapter with dialogue, and using contractions in historical fiction and fantasy, and
- much more.

Grammar for Fiction Writers

Not your same old boring grammar guide! This book is fun, fast, and focused on writing amazing fiction.

The world of grammar is huge, but fiction writers don't need to know all the nuances to write well. In fact, some of the rules you were taught in English class will actually hurt your fiction writing, not help it.

Grammar for Fiction Writers won't teach you things you don't need to know. It's all about the grammar that's relevant to you as you write your novels and short stories.

Here's what you'll find inside:

- **Punctuation Basics** including the special uses of dashes and ellipses in fiction, common comma problems, how to format your dialogue, and untangling possessives and contractions.
- **Knowing What Your Words Mean and What They Don't** including commonly confused words, imaginary words and phrases, how to catch and strengthen weak words, and using connotation and denotation to add powerful subtext to your writing.
- **Grammar Rules Every Writer Needs to Know and Follow** such as maintaining an active voice and making the best use of all the tenses for fast-paced writing that feels immediate and draws the reader in.
- **Special Challenges for Fiction Writers** like reversing cause and effect, characters who are unintentionally doing the impossible, and orphaned dialogue and pronouns.
- **Grammar "Rules" You Can Safely Ignore When Writing Fiction**

Point of View in Fiction

It's the opinions and judgments that color everything the reader believes about the world and the story. It's the voice of the character that becomes as familiar to the reader as their own. It's what makes the story real, believable, and honest.

Yet, despite its importance, point-of-view errors are the most common problem for fiction writers.

In *Point of View in Fiction: A Busy Writer's Guide*, you'll learn...

- the strengths and weaknesses of the four different points of view you can choose for your story (first person, second person, limited third person, and omniscient),
- how to select the right point of view for your story,
- how to maintain a consistent point of view throughout your story,
- practical techniques for identifying and fixing head-hopping and other point-of-view errors,
- the criteria to consider when choosing the viewpoint character for each individual scene or chapter,
- and much more!

FICTION

Frozen: Two Suspenseful Short Stories

Twisted sleepwalking.

A frozen goldfish in a plastic bag.

And a woman afraid she's losing her grip on reality.

"A Purple Elephant" is a suspense short story about grief and betrayal.

In "The Replacements," a prodigal returns home to find that her parents have started a new family, one with no room for her. This disturbing suspense short story is about the lengths to which we'll go to feel like we're wanted, and how we don't always see things the way they really are.

ABOUT THE AUTHOR

Marcy Kennedy is a science fiction, fantasy, and suspense author, freelance editor, and writing instructor who believes there's always hope. Sometimes you just have to dig a little harder to find it. In a world that can be dark and brutal and unfair, hope is one of our most powerful weapons.

She writes novels that encourage people to keep fighting. She wants to let them know that no one is beyond redemption and that, in the end, good always wins.

She writes books for writers to give them the courage to keep trying. She wants to let them know that they can achieve their dream of creating fantastic stories.

She's also a proud Canadian and the proud wife of a former U.S. Marine; owns four cats, two birds, and a dog who weighs as much as she does; and plays board games and the flute (not at the same time). Sadly, she's also addicted to coffee and jelly beans.

You can find her blogging at www.marcykennedy.com about writing and about the place where real life meets science fiction, fantasy, and myth. To sign up for her new-release mailing list, please go to the link below. Not only will you hear about new releases before anyone else, but you'll also receive exclusive discounts and freebies. Your email address will never be shared, and you can unsubscribe at any time.

Newsletter: http://eepurl.com/Bk2Or
Website: www.marcykennedy.com
Email: marcykennedy@gmail.com
Facebook: www.facebook.com/MarcyKennedyAuthor

Made in the USA
Las Vegas, NV
04 February 2024

85225536R00089